REVISE AQA GCSE (9–1)
English Language
MODEL ANSWER WORKBOOK

Series Consultant: Harry Smith
Author: David Grant

Also available to support your revision:

Revise GCSE Study Skills Guide   9781447967071

The **Revise GCSE Study Skills Guide** is full of tried-and-trusted hints and tips for how to learn more effectively. It gives you techniques to help you achieve your best – throughout your GCSE studies and beyond!

Revise GCSE Revision Planner   9781447967828

The **Revise GCSE Revision Planner** helps you to plan and organise your time, step-by-step, throughout your GCSE revision. Use this book and wall chart to mastermind your revision.

For the full range of Pearson revision titles across KS2, KS3, GCSE, Functional Skills, AS/A Level and BTEC visit:
www.pearsonschools.co.uk/revise

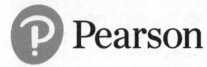

Contents

1   About your exam
2   Command words and mark schemes
3   How to use this book

Paper 1: Explorations in Creative Reading and Writing

Section A: Reading

4   Source A – 20th century prose fiction
5   Source B – 20th century prose fiction
6   Paper 1, Question 1
9   Paper 1, Question 2
15   Paper 1, Question 3
21   Paper 1, Question 4

Section B: Writing

28   Paper 1, Question 5

Paper 2: Writers' Viewpoints and Perspectives

Section A: Reading

40   Source C – 21st century non-fiction
41   Source D – 19th century non-fiction
42   Source E – 21st century non-fiction
43   Source F – 19th century non-fiction
44   Paper 2, Question 1
47   Paper 2, Question 2
53   Paper 2, Question 3
60   Paper 2, Question 4

Section B: Writing

66   Paper 2, Question 5

76   Answers

A small bit of small print:

AQA publishes Sample Assessment Material and the Specification on its website. This is the official content and this book should be used in conjunction with it. The questions and mark schemes have been written to help you practise every topic in the book. Remember: the real exam questions and mark schemes may not look like this.

About your exam

Your AQA (9–1) English Language GCSE comprises **two exam papers.**

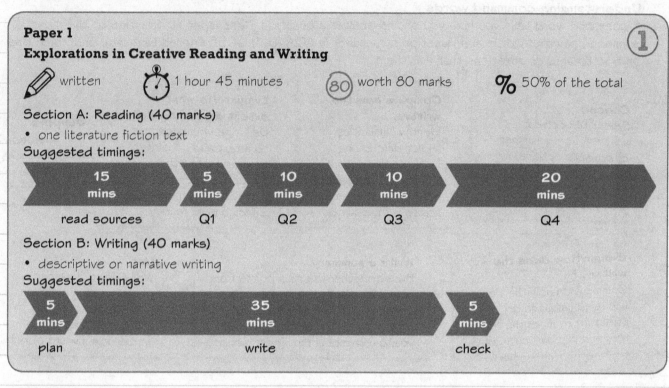

Paper 1
Explorations in Creative Reading and Writing

✏️ written   ⏱️ 1 hour 45 minutes   ⑳ worth 80 marks   % 50% of the total

Section A: Reading (40 marks)

- one literature fiction text

Suggested timings:

15 mins	5 mins	10 mins	10 mins	20 mins
read sources	Q1	Q2	Q3	Q4

Section B: Writing (40 marks)

- descriptive or narrative writing

Suggested timings:

5 mins	35 mins	5 mins
plan	write	check

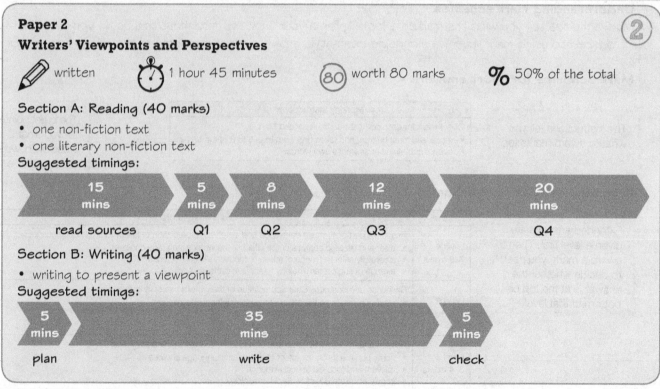

Paper 2
Writers' Viewpoints and Perspectives

✏️ written   ⏱️ 1 hour 45 minutes   ⑳ worth 80 marks   % 50% of the total

Section A: Reading (40 marks)

- one non-fiction text
- one literary non-fiction text

Suggested timings:

15 mins	5 mins	8 mins	12 mins	20 mins
read sources	Q1	Q2	Q3	Q4

Section B: Writing (40 marks)

- writing to present a viewpoint

Suggested timings:

5 mins	35 mins	5 mins
plan	write	check

AQA (9–1) English Language GCSE is not tiered. This means that all students will sit the same exam papers and will have access to the full range of grades.

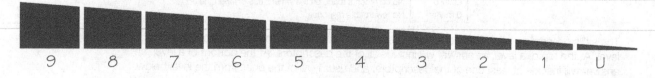

9   8   7   6   5   4   3   2   1   U

Command words and mark schemes

Understanding command words

A command word tells you how you should answer a question. Here is an introduction to the most common command words and question structures in AQA (9–1) GCSE English Language and some tips on how to answer questions that use them.

Choose
Select the correct answers from a number of possible options. You need to shade – not tick or cross – the answers that you think are correct.

Compare how the writers...
Identify similarities and/or differences between the writers' views and ideas, and how those views are put across in the sources.

Evaluate/To what extent do you agree?
Describe your response to a text and consider how successful the writer has been in achieving the intended effect on the reader.

Support
Use quotations and references as evidence for your ideas.

Explain/How does the writer...?
Comment on how the writer has used language or structure to make the reader respond in a particular way.

Write a summary
Bring together the main points from two texts. You'll be asked to write a summary of the differences, the similarities or the details that help you to understand the bigger picture.

List
Write down a number of pieces of information from the text. You can use quotations, your own words or a mixture of both.

Understanding mark schemes

Mark schemes tell you what the marker is looking for in your answer. Throughout this book, you will be introduced to using mark schemes alongside exam-style answers. Here are some of the things to look out for.

Mark schemes for short answers

The instructions tell you what to award marks for.

Marking instructions
Give 1 mark for each point about the Illustrated Man:
• responses must be true, and taken only from lines 5 to 6 of the text
• accept quotations or student's own words.

The bullet points tell you what types of answers are acceptable.

Extended answer mark schemes

Extended answers are given a level first. Then to award a mark, you need to decide whether the answer is at the top or bottom of that level.

Level	Skills descriptors
Level 4 7–8 marks	Response demonstrates a developed and insightful appreciation of the writer's use of language: • clear and detailed analysis of the effect of the writer's language choices • a carefully selected range of relevant, focused textual evidence • a range of subject terminology to achieve clarity and precision.
Level 3 5–6 marks	Response demonstrates clear appreciation of the writer's use of language: • clear comments on the effect of the writer's language choices • a range of relevant, focused textual evidence • a range of subject terminology to achieve clarity.
Level 2 3–4 marks	Response demonstrates some appreciation of the writer's use of language: • some comments on the effect of the writer's language choices • relevant and focused textual evidence • largely accurate use of subject terminology.
Level 1 1–2 marks	Response demonstrates some awareness of the writer's use of language: • straightforward comments on the effect of the writer's language choices • largely relevant textual evidence • some use of subject terminology, with inconsistent accuracy.
Level 0 0 marks	No comments made on the writer's use of language. No rewardable response.

The skills descriptors are a guide to the features that an answer must include to achieve each level. At the top of a level, an answer will include all of the descriptors. At the bottom of a level, an answer will include at least one of the descriptors, and usually all of the ones from the level below.

How to use this book

In this book, you will familiarise yourself with the AQA (9–1) English Language GCSE by engaging with exam-style questions, answers and mark schemes. Doing so means you will know exactly what to expect in the exam and, just as importantly, what will be expected of you.

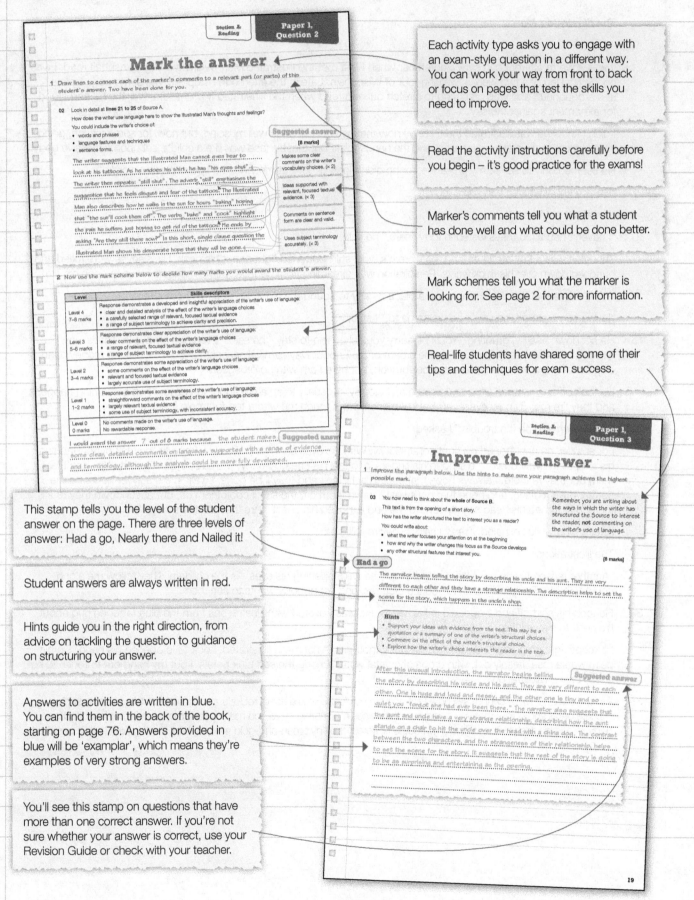

Each activity type asks you to engage with an exam-style question in a different way. You can work your way from front to back or focus on pages that test the skills you need to improve.

Read the activity instructions carefully before you begin – it's good practice for the exams!

Marker's comments tell you what a student has done well and what could be done better.

Mark schemes tell you what the marker is looking for. See page 2 for more information.

Real-life students have shared some of their tips and techniques for exam success.

This stamp tells you the level of the student answer on the page. There are three levels of answer: Had a go, Nearly there and Nailed it!

Student answers are always written in red.

Hints guide you in the right direction, from advice on tackling the question to guidance on structuring your answer.

Answers to activities are written in blue. You can find them in the back of the book, starting on page 76. Answers provided in blue will be 'examplar', which means they're examples of very strong answers.

You'll see this stamp on questions that have more than one correct answer. If you're not sure whether your answer is correct, use your Revision Guide or check with your teacher.

Source A

This extract is from the prologue to a collection of science-fiction short stories by Ray Bradbury.

The Illustrated Man

It was a warm afternoon in early September when I first met the Illustrated Man. Walking along an asphalt road, I was on the final leg of a two weeks' walking tour of Wisconsin. Late in the afternoon I stopped, ate some pork, beans, and a doughnut, and was preparing to stretch out and read when the Illustrated Man walked over the hill and stood for a moment against the sky.

5   I didn't know he was Illustrated then, I only know that he was tall, once well muscled, but now, for some reason, going to fat. I recall that his arms were long, and the hands thick, but that his face was like a child's, set upon a massive body.

He seemed only to sense my presence, for he didn't look directly at me when he spoke his first words.

"Do you know where I can find a job?"

"I'm afraid not," I said.

10   "I haven't had a job that's lasted in forty years," he said.

Though it was a hot late afternoon, he wore his wool shirt buttoned tight about his neck. His sleeves were rolled and buttoned down over his thick wrists. Perspiration was streaming from his face, yet he made no move to open his shirt.

"Well," he said at last, "this is as good a place as any to spend the night. Do you mind company?"

"I have some extra food you'd be welcome to," I said.

15   He sat down heavily, grunting. 'You'll be sorry you asked me to stay," he said. "Everyone always is. That's why I'm walking. Here it is, early September, the cream of the Labour Day carnival season. I should be making money hand over fist at any small town side show celebration, but here I am with no prospects."

He took off an immense shoe and peered at it closely. "I usually keep a job about ten days. Then something happens and they fire me. By now every carnival in America won't touch me with a ten-foot pole."

20   "What seems to be the trouble," I asked.

For answer, he unbuttoned his tight collar, slowly. With his eyes shut, he put a slow hand to the task of unbuttoning his shirt all the way down. He slipped his fingers in to feel his chest. "Funny," he said, eyes still shut. 'You can't feel them but they're there. I always hope that someday I'll look and they'll be gone. I walk in the sun for hours on the hottest days, baking, and hope that my sweat'll wash them off, the sun'll cook them off, but at sundown they're still
25   there." He turned his head slightly toward me and exposed his chest. "Are they still there now?"

After a long while I exhaled. "Yes," I said. "They're still there."

The Illustrations.

"Another reason I keep my collar buttoned up," he said, opening his eyes, "is the children. They follow me along country roads. Everyone wants to see the pictures, and yet nobody wants to see them."

30   He took his shirt off and wadded it in his hands. He was covered with Illustrations from the blue tattooed ring about his neck to his belt line.

"It keeps right on going," he said, guessing my thought. "All of me is Illustrated. Look." He opened his hand. On his palm was a rose, freshly cut, with drops of crystal water among the soft pink petals. I put my hand out to touch it, but it was only an Illustration.

35   As for the rest of him, I cannot say how I sat and stared, for he was a riot of rockets and fountains and people, in such intricate detail and colour that you could hear the voices murmuring small and muted, from the crowds that inhabited his body. When his flesh twitched, the tiny mouths flickered, the tiny green-and-gold eyes winked, the tiny pink hands gestured.

Source B

This extract is from a short story by Dylan Thomas.

A Story

If you can call it a story. There's no real beginning or end and there's very little in the middle. It is all about a day's outing, by charabanc[1] to Porthcawl, which, of course, the charabanc never reached, and it happened when I was so high and much nicer.

I was staying at the time with my uncle and his wife. Although she was my aunt, I never thought of her as anything but
5   the wife of my uncle, partly because he was so big and trumpeting and red-hairy and used to fill every inch of the hot little house like an old buffalo squeezed into an airing cupboard, and partly because she was so small and silk and quick and made no noise at all as she whisked about on padded paws, dusting the china dogs, feeding the buffalo, setting the mousetraps that never caught her; and once she sneaked out of the room, to squeak in a nook or nibble in the hayloft, you forgot she had ever been there.

10   But there he was, always, a steaming hulk of an uncle, his braces straining like hawsers, crammed behind the counter of the tiny shop at the front of the house, and breathing like a brass band; or guzzling and blustery in the kitchen over his gutsy supper, too big for everything except the great black boats of his boots. As he ate, the house grew smaller; he billowed out over the furniture, the loud check meadow of his waistcoat littered, as though after a picnic, with cigarette ends, peelings, cabbage stalks, birds' bones, gravy; and the forest fire of his hair crackled among the hooked hams from
15   the ceiling. She was so small she could hit him only if she stood on a chair, and every Saturday night at half-past ten he would lift her up, under his arm, onto a chair in the kitchen so that she could hit him on the head with whatever was handy, which was always a china dog. On Sundays, and when pickled, he sang high tenor, and had won many cups.

The first I heard of the annual outing was when I was sitting one evening on a bag of rice behind the counter, under one of my uncle's stomachs, reading an advertisement for sheep-dip, which was all there was to read. The shop was
20   full of my uncle, and when Mr. Benjamin Franklyn, Mr. Weazley, Noah Bowen, and Will Sentry came in, I thought it would burst. It was like all being together in a drawer that smelt of cheese and turps, and twist tobacco and sweet biscuits and snuff and waistcoat. Mr. Benjamin Franklyn said that he had collected enough money for the charabanc and twenty cases of pale ale and a pound apiece over that he would distribute among the members of the outing when they first stopped for refreshment, and he was about sick and tired, he said, of being followed by Will Sentry.

25   'All day long, wherever I go,' he said, 'he's after me like a collie with one eye. I got a shadow of my own and a dog. I don't need no Tom, Dick or Harry pursuing me with his dirty muffler on.'

Will Sentry blushed and said, 'It's only oily. I got a bicycle.'

'A man has no privacy at all,' Mr Franklyn went on. 'I tell you he sticks so close I'm afraid to go out the back in case I sit in his lap. It's a wonder to me,' he said, 'he don't follow me into bed at night.'

30   'Wife won't let,' Will Sentry said.

And that started Mr Franklyn off again and they tried to soothe him down by saying: 'Don't you mind Will Sentry' ... 'No harm in old Will' ... 'He's only keeping an eye on the money, Benjie.'

'Aren't I honest?' asked Mr Franklyn in surprise. There was no answer for some time, then Noah Bowen said: 'You know what the committee is. Ever since Bob the Fiddle they don't feel safe with a new treasurer.'

35   'Do you think I'm going to drink the outing funds, like Bob the Fiddle did?' said Mr Franklyn.

'You might,' said my uncle slowly.

'I resign,' said Mr Franklyn.

'Not with our money, you won't,' Will Sentry said.

'Who put dynamite in the salmon pool?' said Mr Weazley, but nobody took any notice of him. And, after a time, they all
40   began to play cards in the thickening dusk of the hot, cheesy shop, and my uncle blew and bugled whenever he won, and Mr Weazley grumbled like a dredger, and I fell to sleep on the gravy-scented mountain meadow of uncle's waistcoat.

Glossary:

charabanc[1] – an early form of bus, either motorised or horse-drawn, often used for sight-seeing trips

Complete the question

1 There are several parts missing from this exam question. Use Source A on page 4 and the student's answers below to help you complete the question.

> **Hints**
> - Think about who or what all the information in the answers is about.
> - Highlight the information related to the answers in the source. This will help you to work out which lines should be specified in the question.

01 Read again the first part of Source A from **lines** .... **to** ....

List .... things from this part of the text about ....
.... **[4 marks]**

Nailed it!

1 It was a warm afternoon. ....

2 It was early September. ....

3 He had been walking along an asphalt road. ....

4 He had stopped to eat some pork, beans and a doughnut. ....

> Only information from the specified section of the text will be credited.

2 There are several parts missing from this exam question. Use Source A on page 4 and the student's answers below to help you complete the question.

01 Read again the .... part of Source A from **lines** .... **to** ....

List .... things from this part of the text about .... **[4 marks]**

Nailed it!

1 One is of a freshly cut rose. ....

2 They are "a riot of rockets and fountains and people". ....

3 They are very intricately detailed. ....

4 They seem to move when his flesh twitches. ....

> Both quoted and paraphrased information will be credited.

Mark the answer

1 A student has written an answer to this question. Use Source A on page 4 and the marking instructions below to decide how many marks you would award the answer.

---

01 Read again the second part of Source A from **lines 5 to 6**.

List **four** things from this part of the text about the Illustrated Man.

[4 marks]

1 The narrator did not know he was illustrated.

2 He is tall.

3 He was once well muscled but is now going to fat.

4 He does not look directly at the narrator when he speaks.

> When you have written your answer, re-read the question. Then re-read the lines in the Source, and finally re-read your answer to make sure you've found the correct answers.

Marking instructions
Give 1 mark for each point about the Illustrated Man: • responses must be true, and taken only from lines 5 to 6 of the text   • accept quotations or student's own words.

I would award the answer .... out of 4 marks because ....

....

....

---

2 A student has written an answer to this question. Use the marking instructions below to decide how many marks you would award the answer.

---

01 Read again the second part of Source A from lines **10 to 12**.

List **four** things from this part of the text about the Illustrated Man.

[4 marks]

1 He hasn't had a job for forty years.

2 He is wearing a wool shirt.

3 He has thick wrists.

4 Perspiration is streaming from his face.

Marking instructions
Give 1 mark for each point about the Illustrated Man: • responses must be true, and taken only from lines 10 to 12 of the text   • accept quotations or student's own words.

I would award the answer .... out of 4 marks because ....

....

....

Build the answer

1 Look at the question below and Source B on page 5. Which quotations would you use in your response? Tick them.

---

01   Read again the second part of Source B from **lines 4 to 9**.

Lista **four** things from this part of the text about the narrator's aunt.   **[4 marks]**

☐ A   I was staying at the time with my uncle and his wife.

☐ B   Although she was my aunt, I never thought of her as anything but the wife of my uncle

☐ C   partly because he was so big and trumpeting and red-hairy

☐ D   and used to fill every inch of the hot little house
      like an old buffalo squeezed into an airing cupboard

☐ E   and partly because she was so small

☐ F   and silk

☐ G   and quick

☐ H   and made no noise at all as she whisked about on padded paws

☐ I   dusting the china dogs

☐ J   feeding the buffalo

☐ K   setting the mousetraps that never caught her

☐ L   and once she sneaked out of the room, to squeak in a nook
      or nibble in the hayloft, you forgot she had ever been there.

When you're answering questions like this, always underline the
command word in the question. It will help you focus your answer
on what the question is asking rather than what you want it to ask.

2 Look at the quotations you have **not** ticked. Explain why you would **not** include each one in
your response.

....

....

....

Complete the question

1 There are several parts missing from this exam question. Use Source A on page 4 and the extracts from the three student responses below to complete the question.

02 Look in detail at **lines** .... **to** .... of Source A.

How does the writer use language here to ....

You could include the writer's choice of:

- words and phrases
- language features and techniques
- sentence forms.

I always highlight the part of the Source I'm being asked to write about before answering the question.

[8 marks]

Nailed it!

Student A
The writer presents the Illustrated Man as a mysterious character, describing his "wool shirt" being buttoned "tight" around his neck with his sleeves "rolled and buttoned down" even though it is a hot day. These descriptive adjectives and phrases create intrigue and make the reader speculate about why the Illustrated Man is dressed in this way and what he might be hiding.

Student B
The Illustrated Man is shown as a huge person who might have once looked impressive. The writer uses a range of adjectives to describe him as "tall" and "once well muscled" with "long" arms and "thick" hands. These adjectives give the impression of a vast, strong man, which could suggest that he is a threatening or dangerous character to meet in an isolated place like this.

Student C
The writer compares his face to "a child's" suggesting he is young at heart or perhaps innocent like a child and not worried about the troubles and problems he has faced in his life. This contrast with his huge body makes him a strange and interesting character for the reader.

2 Use the extracts from the three student responses below to complete this question.

02 Look in detail at **lines** .... **to** .... of Source A.

How does the writer use language here to ....

You could include the writer's choice of:

- words and phrases
- language features and techniques
- sentence forms.

[8 marks]

Nailed it!

Student A
The writer describes how he undoes his shirt "slowly" then with a "slow hand". This repetition emphasises how reluctant he feels about showing his tattoos.

Student B
The Illustrated Man explains that he walks for hours in the sun hoping that "my sweat'll wash them off, the sun'll cook them off". Repeating this structure emphasises how desperate he feels about wanting to get rid of his tattoos.

Student C
The Illustrated Man ends this explanation by asking "Are they still there now?" This short, simple question using simple, monosyllabic vocabulary adds emphasis to his desperation.

Connect the comments

1 Three students have written answers to Question 2 below. Draw lines to connect the marker's comments to the relevant answers.

02 Look in detail at **lines 5 to 12** of Source A.

How does the writer use language here to present the Illustrated Man?

You could include the writer's choice of:

- words and phrases
- language features and techniques
- sentence forms.

[8 marks]

Student A

The writer uses a simile to describe the Illustrated Man's face, saying that it was "like a child's, set upon a massive body". Putting this contrast at the end of the sentence emphasises how mismatched these two things are, suggesting great strength but also the innocence and honesty of a child.

The response shows some awareness of the writer's use of language and makes some reference to its effect, supported with relevant evidence. However the effect identified is not directly relevant to the focus of the question.

Student B

The writer presents the Illustrated Man as a huge man who has got old and put on quite a lot of weight. It says he has a "massive body" and he was "once well muscled" but is now "going to fat". I don't think that the person telling the story knows why this happened though. I can tell this because he says "for some reason", which shows he doesn't know why.

The response shows some appreciation of a range of the writer's language choices, selecting relevant focused evidence and accurately using subject terminology to comment on its effect. Comments could be developed to analyse the writer's use of language in more detail.

Student C

Throughout this part of the Source you get the impression that the Illustrated Man is hiding something. The writer says he "didn't look directly at me". The adverb "directly" makes me think he is avoiding eye contact because he is hiding something. In the same way, the Illustrated Man has perspiration "streaming from his face" because his shirt is "buttoned tight about his neck" and "buttoned down over his thick wrists." This also makes me think he is hiding something because it emphasises that he does not want to undo his shirt.

The response shows a clear and developed appreciation of the combined impact of the writer's choice of vocabulary and sentence form. This is focused on carefully chosen evidence and its effect is analysed in some detail with accurate use of subject terminology.

Our English teacher told us that the best answers have detailed comments on the **effect** of the writer's choices of words, phrases, language techniques and sentence forms.

Mark the answer

1 Draw lines to connect each of the marker's comments to a relevant part (or parts) of this student's answer. Two have been done for you.

02   Look in detail at **lines 21 to 25** of Source A.

How does the writer use language here to show the Illustrated Man's thoughts and feelings?

You could include the writer's choice of:

- words and phrases
- language features and techniques
- sentence forms.

[8 marks]

The writer suggests that the Illustrated Man cannot even bear to look at his tattoos. As he undoes his shirt, he has "his eyes shut". The writer then repeats: "still shut". The adverb "still" emphasises the suggestion that he feels disgust and fear of the tattoos. The Illustrated Man also describes how he walks in the sun for hours "baking" hoping that "the sun'll cook them off". The verbs "bake" and "cook" highlight the pain he suffers just hoping to get rid of the tattoos. He ends by asking "Are they still there now?" In this short, single clause question the Illustrated Man shows his desperate hope that they will be gone.

> Makes some clear comments on the writer's vocabulary choices. (× 2)

> Ideas supported with relevant, focused textual evidence. (× 3)

> Comments on sentence form are clear and valid.

> Uses subject terminology accurately. (× 3)

2 Now use the mark scheme below to decide how many marks you would award the student's answer.

Level	Skills descriptors
Level 4 7–8 marks	Response demonstrates a developed and insightful appreciation of the writer's use of language: • clear and detailed analysis of the effect of the writer's language choices • a carefully selected range of relevant, focused textual evidence • a range of subject terminology to achieve clarity and precision.
Level 3 5–6 marks	Response demonstrates clear appreciation of the writer's use of language: • clear comments on the effect of the writer's language choices • a range of relevant, focused textual evidence • a range of subject terminology to achieve clarity.
Level 2 3–4 marks	Response demonstrates some appreciation of the writer's use of language: • some comments on the effect of the writer's language choices • relevant and focused textual evidence • largely accurate use of subject terminology.
Level 1 1–2 marks	Response demonstrates some awareness of the writer's use of language: • straightforward comments on the effect of the writer's language choices • largely relevant textual evidence • some use of subject terminology, with inconsistent accuracy.
Level 0 0 marks	No comments made on the writer's use of language. No rewardable response.

I would award the answer .... out of 8 marks because ....

....

....

Build the answer

1 Which of the sentences below could you use in a response to this exam-style question? Tick them.

02 Look in detail at **lines 10 to 17** of Source B.

How does the writer use language here to describe the narrator's uncle?

You could include the writer's choice of:

- words and phrases
- language features and techniques
- sentence forms.

In this type of question, you have to choose some of the writer's language choices and comment on their effect – don't just say what the writer has or hasn't done!

[8 marks]

☐ **A** The description begins by describing him as: "a steaming hulk of an uncle".

☐ **B** The description of the narrator's uncle shows how large, noisy and messy he is.

☐ **C** This shows that he is very tall and probably quite fat.

☐ **D** The noun "hulk" makes it sound like he is huge and the adjective "steaming" makes him sound like a vast, powerful machine giving off steam.

☐ **E** The writer has not used any adverbs in this part of the description.

☐ **F** This long sentence listing all of these details helps to show how he completely fills the room with his body and his noise and his mess.

☐ **G** The adjectives "guzzling" and "blustery" create a vivid impression of the uncle. The word "guzzling" suggests he eats a lot, and "blustery" could suggest he has a bad temper, but both create the impression of a man who fills the room with noise and mess.

☐ **H** The simile "breathing like a brass band" uses alliteration to suggest the noise he makes, showing how even his breathing is deafeningly loud.

2 Look at the sentences you have **not** ticked. Explain why you would **not** include each one in your response.

....
....
....

3 Look again at the sentences you have ticked. Which order (A, B, C etc.) would you put them in to build an effective response to the question?

....

Improve the answer

1   Write an improved answer to the question below. Use the hints to make sure your answer achieves the highest possible mark.

02   Look in detail at **lines 10 to 17** of Source B.

How does the writer use language here to describe the narrator's uncle?

You could include the writer's choice of:

- words and phrases
- language features and techniques
- sentence forms.

[8 marks]

Had a go

The writer gives you the impression that the narrator's uncle is very greedy and a very messy eater. The narrator talks about his big supper and there's a big long list of all the kinds of food he has spilt on his waistcoat. It makes you think he must be a very big man.

Hints

To comment effectively on the writer's use of language, you need to do the following:
- support your ideas with evidence from the text
- comment on the effect of specific words, phrases, language features or sentence forms
- explore the impact of the writer's choices on the reader.

....

....

....

....

....

....

....

....

....

....

....

13

Complete the answer

1 Complete the student's answer to achieve the highest possible mark.

02 Look in detail at **lines 4 to 9** of Source B.

How does the writer use language here to describe the narrator's aunt and uncle?

You could include the writer's choice of:

- words and phrases
- language features and techniques
- sentence forms.

[8 marks]

> **Hints**
> - Remember to use subject terminology.
> - Include a range of evidence. The bullet-pointed list in the question prompts you to do so.
> - The question asks you **how** the writer uses language. You need to analyse its impact on the reader.

In this part of the extract, the writer creates the impression that the uncle is a very loud, ...

very big man. The writer describes him as ....

....

....

....

....

....

In contrast, the aunt is described as ....

....

....

....

....

....

....

The writer lists all the things the aunt does in a long sentence: ....

....

....

....

....

....

Find the answer

1 A student has written three points in response to the question below. Which point would you **not** include in your answer? Explain your choice.

03   You now need to think about the **whole** of **Source A**.

This text is from the prologue to a series of short stories.

How has the writer structured the text to interest you as a reader?

You could write about:

- what the writer focuses your attention on at the beginning
- how and why the writer changes this focus as the Source develops
- any other structural features that interest you.

[8 marks]

> Remember – this question is about the ideas the writer has chosen to use and how he has structured them to interest the reader.

Point A	At the start of the Source the writer describes the narrator's very ordinary sounding day: he is on a walking tour and stops to eat "pork, beans and a doughnut". This makes the tattooed man who appears and talks to him seem even more strange and surprising.
Point B	The Illustrated Man explains that "Everyone wants to see the pictures, and yet nobody wants to see them." The two clauses in this sentence are similar in structure but opposite in meaning. This suggests that the tattoos are fascinating but can also be frightening.
Point C	The descriptions of the tattoos at the end of the Source make the reader realise how unusual, even magical, this man's illustrations are. The whole Source has been structured to encourage the reader to want to find out more about the Illustrated Man.

I would not include point .... because ....

....

2 A different student has written three points in response to the same question. Which point would you **not** include in your answer? Explain your choice.

Point A	Throughout the Source, the writer gives the reader limited information to make them ask lots of questions. For example, why can't the Illustrated Man keep a job for more than ten days? Why is he covered in tattoos? The reader is encouraged to keep reading to find out the answers.
Point B	The writer introduces the idea of an Illustrated Man in the very first sentence, which immediately suggests that it will be dramatic when the narrator meets him. Calling him the Illustrated Man and not using his name makes him sound mysterious and intriguing.
Point C	The Illustrated Man asks the question "Are they still there now?", which suggests that he is frightened of his own tattoos – too frightened even to look at them. The short, simple sentence form adds to this impression of fear, as though he is frightened to ask it.

I would not include point .... because ....

....

15

Connect the comments

1 Three students have written answers to the following question. Draw lines to connect each of the marker's comments to the relevant extract.

03 You now need to think about the **whole** of **Source A**.

This text is from the prologue to a series of short stories.

How has the writer structured the text to interest you as a reader?

You could write about:

- what the writer focuses your attention on at the beginning
- how and why the writer changes this focus as the Source develops
- any other structural features that interest you.

[8 marks]

> To answer this type of question effectively, you need to write about what the reader is thinking and feeling as they read the Source.

Extract A

Most of the story is about describing the Illustrated Man, which makes it interesting. It is the way the writer describes him that makes him interesting, describing how he looks and what his tattoos look like. He is a strange man who is covered in all kinds of weird tattoos and so you want to find out why he is covered in them and what they all are and why he cannot keep a job for more than 10 days.

> The response shows some awareness of structural features, making straightforward comments on their effect, with some relevant references to examples from the text.

Extract B

The writer builds up a feeling of mystery for the reader in the first half of the Source. The Illustrated Man's shirt is tightly buttoned on a hot day and he will not look directly at the narrator. It is not until about halfway through the Source that the reader finds out why he is called the Illustrated Man. Even by the end of the Source the reader does not know why he is covered in tattoos or if this is why he cannot keep a job for very long. It keeps the reader guessing.

> The response shows some appreciation of structural features, identifying a range of relevant, focused examples from the Source and making some comment on their effect.

Extract C

In the short opening paragraph, the writer focuses on the narrator. We are given details about when the story takes place, what the narrator is doing, what he is eating and what he is about to do. These are the kind of details you expect at the start of a story, helping to set a very normal scene, which makes the appearance of a very abnormal character like the Illustrated Man seem even more dramatic as he walks over the hill and "stood for a moment against the sky."

> The response shows a clear appreciation of structural features and their impact on the reader, which are analysed in detail and supported with a carefully selected range of relevant, focused examples.

Mark the answer

1 Draw lines to connect each of the marker's comments to a relevant part (or parts) of this student's answer.

---

03 You now need to think about the **whole** of **Source A**.

This text is from the prologue to a series of short stories.

How has the writer structured the text to interest you as a reader?

You could write about:

- what the writer focuses your attention on at the beginning
- how and why the writer changes this focus as the Source develops
- any other structural features that interest you.

[8 marks]

The extract finishes by focusing on the Illustrated Man's tattoos,

which is what the opening has been building up to all along.

The writer emphasises how realistic they are when the narrator

reaches out to touch the rose, describing its "soft pink petals"

then realising it was "only an illustration". The tattoos then

become stranger and more disturbing because they seem to be

moving. This makes you want to find out more about them.

> Relevant, focused example. (×2)

> Some comment on the effect of the writer's use of a structural feature.

> Accurate use of subject terminology.

> The effect of this structural feature could be explored in more depth.

---

2 Now use the mark scheme below to decide how many marks you would award this student's answer.

Level	Skills descriptors
Level 4 7–8 marks	Response demonstrates a developed and insightful appreciation of structural features: • clear and detailed analysis of the effect of the writer's use of structural features • a carefully selected range of relevant, focused examples • a range of subject terminology to achieve clarity and precision.
Level 3 5–6 marks	Response demonstrates clear appreciation of structural features: • clear comments on the effect of the writer's use of structural features • a range of relevant, focused examples • a range of subject terminology to achieve clarity.
Level 2 3–4 marks	Response demonstrates some appreciation of structural features: • some comments on the effect of the writer's use of structural features • relevant and focused examples • largely accurate use of subject terminology.
Level 1 1–2 marks	Response demonstrates some awareness of structural features: • straightforward comments on the effect of the writer's use of structural features • largely relevant examples • some use of subject terminology, with inconsistent accuracy.
Level 0 0 marks	No comments made on the writer's use of structure. No rewardable response.

I would award the answer .... out of 8 marks because ....

....

....

Build the answer

1 Look at the question below and Source B on page 5. Which sentences would you use in your response? Tick them.

---

03 You now need to think about the **whole** of **Source B**.

This text is from the opening of a short story.

How has the writer structured the text to interest you as a reader?

You could write about:

- what the writer focuses your attention on at the beginning
- how and why the writer changes this focus as the Source develops
- any other structural features that interest you. **[8 marks]**

☐ **A** The story has a very weird beginning.

☐ **B** The writer talks directly to the reader, beginning "If you can call it a story".

☐ **C** This immediately engages the reader's attention and their curiosity, making you wonder how this story, which is called "A Story", is not really a story.

☐ **D** This makes you think it may not be worth reading the story because it is not a proper story.

☐ **E** The writer also tells you how the story will end, explaining that the charabanc "never reached" Porthcawl, so even though you know what will not happen, you want to find out what will happen and why the outing went wrong.

☐ **F** The writer uses humour in this first paragraph to entertain the reader by being hard on himself and on the story.

☐ **G** He says that the story has "no real beginning or end and there's very little in the middle" and that the story happened when he was "so high", meaning he was a child, and "much nicer." This makes you wonder what kind of story this will be and what kind of person is telling it.

☐ **H** The surprising and unusual opening introduces the story and the narrator, using a very small amount of information and some humour to engage the reader's interest.

---

2 Look again at the sentences you have ticked. Which order (A, B, C etc.) would you put them in to build an effective response to the question?

....

Improve the answer

1 Improve the paragraph below. Use the hints to make sure your paragraph achieves the highest possible mark.

03   You now need to think about the **whole** of **Source B**.

This text is from the opening of a short story.

How has the writer structured the text to interest you as a reader?

You could write about:

- what the writer focuses your attention on at the beginning
- how and why the writer changes this focus as the Source develops
- any other structural features that interest you.

> Remember, you are writing about the ways in which the writer has structured the Source to interest the reader, **not** commenting on the writer's use of language.

[8 marks]

Had a go

The narrator begins telling the story by describing his uncle and his aunt. They are very different to each other and they have a strange relationship. The description helps to set the scene for the story, which happens in the uncle's shop.

Hints

- Support your ideas with evidence from the text. This may be a quotation or a summary of one of the writer's structural choices.
- Comment on the effect of the writer's structural choice.
- Explore how the writer's choice interests the reader in the text.

....
....
....
....
....
....
....
....
....
....
....

Complete the answer

1 Complete the student's answer to achieve the highest possible mark.

03 You now need to think about the **whole** of **Source B**.

This text is from the opening of a short story.

How has the writer structured the text to interest you as a reader?

You could write about:

- what the writer focuses your attention on at the beginning
- how and why the writer changes this focus as the Source develops
- any other structural features that interest you.

[8 marks]

Hints

- Your answer should focus on the text at a structural level, not at a language level.
- Use the bullet-pointed list in the question to help you structure your answer.
- Remember to use subject terminology.

In the first paragraph of the story, the writer grabs the reader's interest ....

....

....

....

....

....

....

The writer then goes on to describe ....

....

....

....

....

....

The story then moves on to describe the evening when his uncle's friends come to visit. The

writer introduces conflict between the friends ....

....

....

....

....

....

Complete the question

1 There are several parts missing from this exam question. Use Source A on page 4 and the extracts from the three student responses below to complete the question.

---

04 Focus this part of your answer on the .... part of Source A from line .... to ....

A student, having read this section of the text said: " ....

.... "

To what extent do you agree?

In your response, you could:

- write about your own impressions of ....
- evaluate how the writer has created these impressions
- support your opinions with references to the text.

[20 marks]

Nailed it!

Student A

The first way in which the writer makes the tattoos seem fascinating is the description of the rose, which is so realistic that the narrator thinks he can touch it. The writer effectively describes it as though it were a real rose, writing that it has been "freshly cut" with "drops of crystal water" on its "soft pink petals". The writer not only goes into detail about what the rose looks like but also how it feels, which shows the reader how realistic it looks. This description makes you think that they must be very good tattoos, or perhaps that there is something strange or magical about them.

Student B

Although the writer's description of the tattoos themselves is interesting, it is the way in which the effect that they have had on the Illustrated Man's life is explained that makes them really fascinating and equally disturbing. Even before the reader finds out what they look like, the writer makes it clear that they have ruined this man's life. The reader finds out that children follow the Illustrated Man around and that he can only "keep a job about ten days". All of these details are effective in making you realise that there is something disturbing about the tattoos.

Student C

The writer's clear and detailed description of the way the people in the tattoos seem to be moving makes them fascinating and disturbing. The writer lists all the different movements the narrator sees in a series of clauses to suggest them all moving at the same time: the flesh "twitched", the mouths "flickered", the eyes "winked" and the hands "gestured". These action verbs vividly create the impression of small movements adding up to the impression of a constantly changing picture. The writer also describes the "crowds that inhabited his body". The verb "inhabited" is a kind of personification that brings the images to life, suggesting that they are living people who live on the Illustrated Man's skin, which is the most disturbing idea in the whole extract.

Find the answer

1 A student has written three paragraphs in response to the question below. Which paragraph would you include in your answer? Explain your choice. Then, explain why you would **not** include the other two paragraphs.

04   Focus this part of your answer on the second part of Source A from **line 18 to the end**.

A student, having read this section of the text said: "The writer makes you feel sorry for the Illustrated Man. You can see why his tattoos have caused him so many problems."

To what extent do you agree?

In your response, you could:

- write about your own impressions of the Illustrated Man and his tattoos
- evaluate how the writer has created these impressions
- support your opinions with references to the text.   [20 marks]

> Evaluation questions like this usually ask you to focus on half the Source, so make sure you only include in your answer references from the relevant part of the text.

Paragraph A
The writer is successful in making you feel sorry for the Illustrated Man by explaining how desperately the Illustrated Man is trying to keep his tattoos covered up. The writer effectively shows how hot it is, describing the Man's perspiration "streaming from his face", and emphasises that he is wearing a thick, warm "wool" shirt, which is "buttoned tight" around his neck and "buttoned down" around his wrists. In this way the writer makes it obvious that the Illustrated Man wants to keep himself covered up because he has something to hide.

Paragraph B
The writer describes the tattoos as "a riot of rockets and fountains and people". The metaphor "a riot" makes it sound like there are hundreds of tattoos crowded together, fighting for space. The description contrasts "rockets", which suggest power and violence with "fountains", which suggest peace and beauty, showing how different all the tattoos are. It's as if the man is illustrated with a whole world of tattoos.

Paragraph C
The writer most successfully makes the reader feel sorry for the Illustrated Man when he writes about how the Illustrated Man has tried to remove his tattoos. He describes walking "for hours" and "baking" hoping that his "sweat'll wash them off, the sun'll cook them off", which shows the pain he is prepared to go through to try to get rid of them. However, the reader knows this will not work, which makes the Illustrated Man seem even more hopeless and trapped by his tattoos.

I would include paragraph .... because ....

....

....

....

I would not include paragraphs .... or .... because ....

....

....

....

Mark the answer

1 Draw lines to connect each of the marker's comments to a relevant part of this student's answer.

04 Focus this part of your answer on the second part of Source A from **line 18 to the end**.

A student, having read this section of the text said: "The writer's description of the tattoos makes them fascinating but also disturbing. It is as if they are alive."

To what extent do you agree?

In your response, you could:

- write about your own impressions of the Illustrated Man's tattoos
- evaluate how the writer has created these impressions
- support your opinions with references to the text.

[20 marks]

The description of the tattoos is fascinating from the moment the

Illustrated Man reveals them. The narrator says he is "covered

with illustrations" and describes the "blue tattooed ring about his

neck". The word "ring" makes it sound like a solid line of tattoos all

around his neck, which emphasises how completely he is covered.

The man himself then goes on to say that "All of me is illustrated."

So the first impression you get is of a man who is completely

covered in tattoos from his head to his feet. The writer also

describes them as "a riot", which means there are a lot of them.

> Response is focused on the statement in the question.

> Ideas supported with a range of relevant, focused textual evidence.

> Makes some clear comments on the writer's choices.

> Some effective evaluation of the effect of the writer's choices on the reader.

> Limited evaluation of the effect of the writer's choices on the reader.

2 Now use the mark scheme below to decide how many marks you would award the answer.

Level	Skills descriptors	
Level 4 16–20 marks	Response demonstrates developed and insightful evaluation: • clear and detailed analysis of the writer's choices • clear and full evaluation of the effect on the reader	• a carefully selected range of relevant, focused textual evidence • a developed and considered critical response to the statement.
Level 3 11–15 marks	Response demonstrates clear and focused evaluation: • clear comments on the writer's choices • clear evaluation of the effect on the reader	• a range of relevant, focused textual evidence • a relevant, focused response to the statement.
Level 2 6–10 marks	Response demonstrates inconsistently focused evaluation: • some comments on the writer's choices • some evaluation of their effect on the reader	• relevant and focused textual evidence • a more developed response to the statement.
Level 1 1–5 marks	Response demonstrates limited, straightforward evaluation: • straightforward comments on the writer's choices • straightforward evaluation of their effect on the reader	• largely relevant textual evidence • a straightforward response to the statement.
Level 0 0 marks	No comments made on the writer's choices, no evaluation, and no response to the statement. No rewardable response.	

I would award the answer .... out of 20 marks because

....

....

....

Connect the comments

1 Three students have written answers to the following question. Draw lines to connect each of the marker's comments to the relevant extract.

04 Focus this part of your answer on the second part of Source A from **line 18 to the end**.

A student, having read this section of the text said: "The writer makes you feel sorry for the Illustrated Man. You can see why his tattoos have caused him so many problems."

To what extent do you agree?

In your response, you could:

- write about your own impressions of the Illustrated Man and his tattoos
- evaluate how the writer has created these impressions
- support your opinions with references to the text.

[20 marks]

> **Hint**
> • The best answers give a clear judgement on the success of the writer's choices and their effect.

Extract A

The writer clearly creates the impression that the tattoos cause problems because you cannot help looking at them. For example, the narrator says, "I cannot say how I sat and stared", which suggests he was hypnotised by the "intricate detail and colour" of the tattoos, and believes he can hear their voices "murmuring" as they "twitched" and "gestured". The writer is beginning to show why "Everyone wants to see the pictures" but also why "nobody wants to see them" because there is something disturbing about the way they appear to move and speak.

The response makes some straightforward comments on the writer's choice, supported with relevant reference to the Source. There is some reference to the statement but with only limited evaluation of the text's impact on the reader.

Extract B

I think the writer makes you feel really sorry for the man by describing all the problems that the tattoos have caused. For example, he cannot keep a job and none of the carnivals will touch him "with a ten-foot pole" and he says that "Everyone wants to see the pictures, and yet nobody wants to see them." It creates a strong impression of someone who is lonely and feels rejected.

The response clearly evaluates the text's impact on the reader with some straightforward comments and a range of relevant focused evidence. Comments could be developed to focus more closely on the writer's language choices and how they achieve the effect identified.

Extract C

I feel sorry for the Illustrated Man because he does not like his tattoos. He says he wants to burn them off by walking for hours in the sun, which would be really painful. It shows how much he hates them. He also says he wants his sweat to wash them off, which shows the same thing, and also makes you feel sorry for him.

The response makes a developed evaluation of the text, closely focused on the statement in the question, supported with a range of carefully selected evidence. The impact of the writer's choices is analysed with insight and in some depth.

Build the answer

1 Look at the question below and Source B on page 5. Which sentences would you use in your response? Tick them.

---

04 Focus this part of your answer on the second half of Source B from **line 18 to the end**.

A student, having read this section of the text said: "The writer brings the scene in the shop to life for the reader. It is as if you are in the shop with the narrator and the other characters."

To what extent do you agree?

In your response, you could:

- write about your own impressions of the scene in the shop
- evaluate how the writer has created these impressions
- support your opinions with references to the text.   **[20 marks]**

☐	A	The narrator is reading an advert for sheep-dip, which quickly tells you how bored he is in the shop with his uncle.
☐	B	When the narrator adds that he thought the shop "would burst" it creates a vivid impression of the tiny room, crowded with people.
☐	C	"Mr. Benjamin Franklyn, Mr. Weazley, Noah Bowen, and Will Sentry."
☐	D	The narrator presents all the characters that come into the shop in a long list to emphasise how many of them there are.
☐	E	The narrator lists the names of characters that we do not know in order to confuse the reader.
☐	F	The description using the senses of sight and smell and touch is so vivid that you do feel as though you are there, crammed in a small, dark, smelly shop with the narrator and all his uncle's friends.
☐	G	The writer uses a simile to compare being in the shop to "being together in a drawer" filled with the smell of "cheese and turps, and twist tobacco and sweet biscuits and snuff and waistcoat."
☐	H	Repeating the conjunction "and" in this long list emphasises the strange and horrible mixture of smells, making the room feel even more crowded.

---

2 Look at the sentences you have **not** ticked. Explain why you would **not** include each one in your response.

....

3 Look again at the sentences you have ticked. Which order (A, B, C etc.) would you put them in to build an effective response to the question?

....

Improve the answer

1 Improve the paragraph below. Use the hints to make sure your paragraph achieves the highest possible mark.

04   Focus this part of your answer on the second half of Source B from **line 18 to the end**.

A student, having read this section of the text said: "The writer brings the scene in the shop to life for the reader. It is as if you are in the shop with the narrator and the other characters."

To what extent do you agree?

In your response, you could:

- write about your own impressions of the scene in the shop
- evaluate how the writer has created these impressions
- support your opinions with references to the text.   **[20 marks]**

Had a go

Mr Franklyn says a lot about being followed around by Will Sentry. It makes him sound angry and upset. None of the other characters say very much.

> **Hints**
>
> To write an effective evaluation, you need to do the following:
> - focus on what the writer has done and consider why they have done it.
> - support your ideas with evidence from the text.
> - make a personal judgement on the effectiveness of the writer's choices, referring to the statement in the question.

....
....
....
....
....
....
....
....
....
....
....
....

Complete the answer

1 Complete the student's answer to achieve the highest possible mark.

04 Focus this part of your answer on the second half of Source B from **line 18 to the end**.

A student, having read this section of the text said: "The writer brings the scene in the shop to life for the reader. It is as if you are in the shop with the narrator and the other characters."

To what extent do you agree?

In your response, you could:

- write about your own impressions of the scene in the shop
- evaluate how the writer has created these impressions
- support your opinions with references to the text.

> Remember, you are being asked to what extent you agree. That means you need to form and present an opinion.

[20 marks]

The narrator sets the scene in the shop, describing ....

....

....

....

....

....

....

Mr Franklyn is the first character to speak ....

....

....

....

....

....

....

The other characters try to "soothe" Mr Franklyn. The writer puts all of their dialogue on the

same line ....

....

....

....

....

....

....

....

....

Build the answer

1 Look at this question and the student's ideas below. Which ideas would you use in a plan to answer this question? Tick them.

05 You are going to enter a creative writing competition.

Your entry will be judged by a panel of people of your own age.

Write a description suggested by this picture:

(24 marks for content and organisation
16 marks for technical accuracy)
[40 marks]

	A	The man says he found the dog

	B	Wake up one sunny morning in summer holidays

	C	Decide to walk through woods with dog

	D	Walk to woods down main road – busy traffic

	E	Walking through woods, dog running about excitedly.

	F	Clouds come over... dark and moody sky.

	G	Dog runs off barking... silence

	H	I go look for dog, calling his name

	I	Starting to panic

	J	Feeling like being watched – noises, eyes

	K	Build tension – shadowy figure in distance, beckoning

	L	He's got my dog on a lead

	M	I run to him, shouting give me back my dog

	N	I thank him and go home with my dog

2 Look at the ideas you have **not** ticked. Explain why you would **not** include each one in your response.

....

3 Look again at the ideas you have ticked. Which order (A, B, C etc.) would you put them in to build an effective response to the question?

....

....

Find the answer

1 Which of the openings below would you use to begin your answer to this question? Explain your choice. Then, explain why you would **not** use the other two openings.

05 You are going to enter a creative writing competition.

Your entry will be judged by a panel of people of your own age.

Write a description suggested by this picture:

(24 marks for content and organisation
16 marks for technical accuracy)

[40 marks]

Opening A | The bright golden yellow sun blazed like a ball of furious fire in the pure, blue, perfectly clear, cloudless sky, sending its luminous beams shining down to dance on the glowing green leaves as they rustled and whispered and fluttered in a warm, wafting, breeze that wafted and flitted gently through the lush woodland landscape.

Opening B | It was a nice sunny day. I decided to go for a nice walk in the woods. I got to the woods. I walked through the woods. The woods looked lovely because the sun was shining and the leaves were all green and there were some flowers growing in the grass. All of a sudden, the sun went in and it had got really cloudy. It looked like it was going to rain. There was a cold wind. I shivered a bit.

Opening C | The warm sun beat down on the back of my neck as we reached the woods. I let Dirk the terrier off his lead and smiled as he hurtled into the trees, his nose to the ground and his tail spinning like the blades of a helicopter. I set off along the dusty woodland path, Dirk charging back to me with his tongue hanging nearly to the ground, then charging ahead again to see what else he needed to sniff.

I would use opening .... because ....

....

....

I would not use openings .... or .... because ....

....

....

....

Connect the comments

1 Three students have written answers to the following question. Draw lines to connect each of the marker's comments to the relevant extract.

05 You are going to enter a creative writing competition.

Your entry will be judged by a panel of people of your own age.

Write a description suggested by this picture:

(24 marks for content and organisation
16 marks for technical accuracy)

[40 marks]

Extract A

I ran myself to a standstill, my chest heaving as, clutching a tree, I tried to breathe. Still my eyes scanned the woods looking for any sign of the dog. A flash of her white fur, the sharp crack of a twig, a rustle in the undergrowth. But the woods were silent. Then, in the distance, silhouetted against the sky, I saw a human shape. In the shadows, I could see his eyes, white and staring. They were staring at me.

Limited achievement of descriptive purpose, using simple vocabulary choices and a limited variety of sentence forms. There is some linking of relevant ideas.

Extract B

As I looked into the murky water of the pond I thought I saw a face. It looked like the face of a man. He had a round face with a beard. But what was very strange was that his hair and his beard were all thick and straggly and green. It looked like his hair was made of the pondweed that grew all around the edge of the pond. His mouth was moving like he was trying to say something but obviously he was under the water so I couldn't hear what he was saying.

The response frequently achieves the purpose of description with some effective choices of vocabulary and sentence forms to present a range of relevant, linked ideas.

Extract C

I walked on trying to find the path but I couldn't find it. I didn't know where I was because I was lost. I wanted to go home. I turned around and went in the other direction. Then I came to a big pond which I had never seen before. The water was all brown and dirty. You couldn't see anything in the water because it was so brown and dirty and it smelt funny. Then I heard a voice and I looked up and there was someone watching me. The person called out. I felt a bit frightened.

The response is consistently focused on description using a considerable variety of vocabulary and sentence forms carefully created for effect. Ideas are structured to engage the reader.

Find the answer

1 Look at the student responses to this question. Which response contains no spelling, punctuation or grammar errors? Tick it.

2 Then, cross out and correct any spelling, punctuation or grammar errors in the responses below.

05 You are going to enter a creative writing competition.

Your entry will be judged by a panel of people of your own age.

Write a description suggested by this picture:

> I always save time to check my work at the end of an exam – it's always worth it.

(24 marks for content and organisation
16 marks for technical accuracy)
[40 marks]

☐ A
I broke into a run. My feet were pounding on the forest floor, my heart was pounding in my chest, and I could hardly breath. I kept glancing over my shoulder to see if he was following me, I knew I had to get away from him. When I couldn't run no more, I stopped and turned around. He had dissappeared. There was no sign of him. I began to wonder if I had made a mistake. Perhaps he was just a harmless old man, walking in the woods with his dog. Perhaps I had been silly and panicked when there was no need.

☐ B
Each pebble skimmed across the surface of the pond before sinking without a trace. Ripples spread out across the water, like the rings on a target. I turned and headed deeper into the forest, and its dark, dense canopy of leaves overhead thickened until it felt like night was falling. At the beginning of my walk, the sunlight was almost too bright to bear but now I could hardly see a thing. The trees closed in around me, their thick roots spreading across my path and trying to trip me up in the darkness.

☐ C
Its difficult to get lost in these woods. Their are clearly marked, gravel paths that lead you through the open grassy verges and the deepest, darkest parts of the forest. So you can just relax and enjoy the view from the hill at the top of the woods, were you can see the tiny farms in the vallys below, the mountains in the distance and the tiny cars on the tiny road below. They look like toys and make you feel like a giant.

Mark the answer

1 Draw lines to connect each of the marker's comments to a relevant part (or parts) of this extract from a student's answer. One has been done for you.

05 You are going to enter a creative writing competition.

Your entry will be judged by a panel of people of your own age.

Write a description suggested by this picture:

(24 marks for content and organisation
16 marks for technical accuracy)
[40 marks]

Before my eyes, the swirling clouds of mist thickened and the forest disappeared in a white blanket of fog. The trees, their leaves, the sky were gone. All that I could see was the thick trunks of two trees that were a metre in front of me, and my feet on the stony path below me. I began to walk, blindly following the path, hoping it would lead me to the edge of the forest and back to safety. I peered into the fog, knowing I had no idea where I was or where I was going, scanning the whiteness for a glimpse of something I knew, something I recognised. But when I paused and looked down at my feet again, there was no path, only thick grass and brambles. The path was gone.

Careful vocabulary choice contributes to vivid description.

Effective structural decision, slowly building the feeling of being lost.

Short sentence form crafted for dramatic effect.

Deliberate use of repetition for effect. (× 2)

2 Draw lines to connect each of the marker's comments to a relevant part (or parts) of this extract from a student's answer to the same question. One has been done for you.

I walk around the pond towards the man on the other side. He's quite tall with white hair and he's got serious wrinkles and he's dressed in well old clothes and he's looking across the pond like he hasn't seen me and I tries to talk to him but he just ignores me. I go to tap him on the shoulder. My hand goes straight through him! He's see-through! He's a ghost!

Simple vocabulary choice limits the effectiveness of the description.

Inappropriate use of non-Standard English for this task. (× 3)

Overlong sentence with repetitive structure.

Appropriate choice of punctuation to show narrator's sudden realisation.

Improve the answer

1 Improve the paragraph below. Use the hints to make sure your paragraph achieves the highest possible mark.

05 You are going to enter a creative writing competition.

Your entry will be judged by a panel of people of your own age.

Write a description suggested by this picture:

(24 marks for content and organisation
16 marks for technical accuracy)
[40 marks]

Had a go

It was raining when I got to the pond in the woods. There was a man standing on the other side. He looked a bit scary. I wondered whether to turn around and go back, or maybe I should just keep walking and hope everything would be alright. I felt nervous but I walked round the pond towards him.

Hints

- An effective description should create a vivid image in the reader's mind.
- Aim to describe the scene, and the people in it, so your reader can clearly imagine them.
- Try to describe the feelings of the people in your description. What happens to your mind and your body when you feel nervous?
- Describing the weather can be effective in creating mood or atmosphere.
- Try not to rush through your ideas. Think carefully about how you can bring each moment in your description to life.

....
....
....
....
....
....
....
....
....

Build the answer

1 Look at this question and the student's ideas below. Which ideas would you use in a plan to answer this writing task? Tick them.

The second option for the writing task on Paper 1 may use the command word 'describe', but you can still plan and write it as a story.

05 Describe an occasion when you could not believe your eyes.

Focus on the thoughts and feelings you had at that time.

(24 marks for content and organisation
16 marks for technical accuracy)

[40 marks]

☐ A   There's a big party on Saturday at Laura's house.

☐ B   It's Laura's 16th birthday and she always gets good presents.

☐ C   Laura's got a really nice house and loads of friends.

☐ D   Laura's really nice but quite spoilt!

☐ E   I decide I need to get a new outfit and change my hairstyle.

☐ F   Ring up my friend to come and help me with my hair.

☐ G   We start by colouring it to make it blonder.

☐ H   I wash the colour out. My hair is green.

☐ I   Panic.

☐ J   My friend says I should dry it and see how bad it looks.

☐ K   I dry it. It looks worse. I can't believe it.

☐ L   What do I do? Try again? What if it starts falling out?

☐ M   Do I go to the party with green hair or hide at home?

☐ N   I decide to go to the party. Feeling scared.

☐ O   Standing on Laura's doorstep about to ring the bell. Scared.

☐ P   Walk into the party. Everyone's staring. Really anxious.

☐ Q   Everyone loves my hair at the party. Have a great time.

☐ R   It turned out OK, but I promise myself I will never colour my hair again.

2 Look again at the ideas you have ticked. Which order (A, B, C etc.) would you put them in to build an effective response to the question?

....

....

Connect the comments

1 Three students have written an opening paragraph to the following question. Draw lines to connect each of the marker's comments to the relevant extract.

05 Describe an occasion when you could not believe your eyes.

Focus on the thoughts and feelings you had at that time.

(24 marks for content and organisation
16 marks for technical accuracy)
[40 marks]

Extract A

I woke up one Christmas morning and I ran downstairs to see my presents. I was only seven years old and I was very excited. I knew they would be under the Christmas tree because they always were. I hurried into the front room and saw the Christmas tree but there were no presents under it. I couldn't believe what I was seeing so I went into the kitchen but there weren't any presents in there either. I can remember feeling like I was going to cry because I thought I must have slept for two days and missed Christmas. My mum and dad heard me bawling and howling and came running downstairs.

There is a limited sense of narrative purpose in this opening. There is an attempt to engage the reader through simple vocabulary choices and a limited variety of sentence forms.

Extract B

Once I woke up in the middle of the night and it was dark. I could hear a noise in my room and I felt scared so I closed my eyes tight and lay very still. Then something or someone sat on the end of my bed. Now I was really scared. I opened my eyes and I couldn't believe my eyes. There was a lady sitting on the end of my bed and she was sort of glowing all over and she was smiling at me. I didn't know who she was so I said to her "Who are you?" but she just smiled and didn't say anything.

The ideas in this opening paragraph have been selected to engage the reader, and are effectively developed with some deliberate choices of vocabulary. However, a limited range of sentence forms reduces its full impact.

From the very first engaging sentence to the cliffhanger in the final sentence, ideas are selected, and a considerable variety of vocabulary and sentence forms are carefully crafted, to engage the reader in this well structured opening paragraph.

Extract C

I can remember the time the world first turned white. I was hardly tall enough to see over the windowsill when I pulled back the curtains on a cold, winter morning all those years ago. All I could see was a white sky, and a white street filled with white cars. I blinked and scrunched up my eyes and I remember a feeling of excitement beginning to burn in my stomach. So, this was what my parents meant the night before when they had told me it might snow. Even they seemed excited. But I had no idea what snow looked like. And as I looked out of the window that morning, I realised I had no idea what snow felt like or sounded like. I would soon find out.

Complete the answer

1 Read this question then complete each student's plan by adding an effective ending for each of their stories.

A good story needs to set the scene, involve a conflict or problem that builds up and reaches a crisis, and then provide a resolution or ending to finish it off.

05 Describe an occasion when you could not believe your eyes.

Focus on the thoughts and feelings you had at that time.

(24 marks for content and organisation
16 marks for technical accuracy)

[40 marks]

Student A

- I had been telling everyone for weeks it was nearly my 16ᵗʰ birthday.
- Woke up on my birthday. The house was empty. Note from my mum – "See you later".
- Hung around bored all day. My friend texted: meet me in the park. I went to meet her.
- ....
  ....
  ....

Student B

- Woke up one Christmas morning when I was seven. Ran downstairs to open presents.
- No presents under the tree or anywhere else.
- Mum and Dad came in. It was like they had forgotten it was Christmas.
- ....
  ....
  ....

Student C

- Very excited about going on holiday. Getting on the plane, getting to the hotel.
- The hotel is a dump. It looks like a building site. Our room smells. So disappointed.
- Go to bed that night. Dripping tap. Strange creaking noises.
- ....
  ....
  ....

Re-order the answer

1 The sentences below are taken from a paragraph written by a student in response to the following question. Rearrange the sentences into the most logical order by numbering them from 1 to 5.

> **05** Describe an occasion when you could not believe your eyes.
>
> Focus on the thoughts and feelings you had at that time.
>
> (24 marks for content and organisation
> 16 marks for technical accuracy)
> **[40 marks]**

The first and last sentences of a paragraph are often the most important. The first one can grab the reader, and the last one can make them want to find out what happens next.

☐ As we reached the hotel and got out of the taxi, my heart sank.

☐ But it was even worse than it looked.

☐ Around the hotel, where there should have been grass and flowers, there was rubble and dust.

☐ There were diggers and dumpers and bulldozers everywhere, none of them moving.

☐ I remember wondering whether they hadn't finished building the hotel yet, or whether some of it had recently fallen down.

2 The sentences below are taken from a paragraph written by another student in response to the same question. Rearrange the sentences into the most logical order by numbering them from 1 to 5.

☐ I pushed the pillow up over my ears, closed my eyes as tightly as I could to try to go to sleep.

☐ The thin curtains glowed with the lights from the street outside.

☐ Music from the club next door thumped through the walls and made the floor shake.

☐ Maybe, I thought, I'll wake up in the morning and find that this was all just a bad dream.

☐ I could hear the water in the clanking pipes gurgling and the drip, drip, drip of the tap in the dirty bathroom.

Mark the answer

1 Draw lines to connect each of the marker's comments to a relevant part of this student's answer. One has been done for you.

05   Describe an occasion when you could not believe your eyes.

Focus on the thoughts and feelings you had at that time.

(24 marks for content and organisation
16 marks for technical accuracy)
[40 marks]

Mum held the box down so I could peak in.
I couldn't believe it. In the box were two little
floppy ears, a black nose, and two brown eyes
looking back at me. It was a puppy. She was
wagging her tail like she was really pleased to
see me. And I was delighted to see her!

Full stops and other sentence demarcation are accurate. (You only need to provide one example of this.)

A short, simple sentence is used to express shock.

Vocabulary choices are somewhat varied.

Spelling of some less common words is inaccurate.

2 Now use the mark scheme below to decide how many marks you would award the answer for technical accuracy.

Level	Skills descriptors	
Level 4 13–16 marks	• Sentence demarcation is consistently accurate. • Meaning is fully supported with a range of punctuation, used highly accurately. • Sentence forms are highly varied and crafted for effect.	• Standard English is used consistently and appropriately, with secure management of grammatical structures. • Vocabulary choices are sophisticated. • Spelling is highly accurate.
Level 3 9–12 marks	• Sentence demarcation is usually accurate. • Meaning is usually supported with a range of punctuation, used with some accuracy. • Sentence forms are varied and crafted for effect.	• Standard English is used generally accurately, with largely accurate management of grammatical structures. • A broad range of vocabulary choices is used. • Less common words are generally accurately spelled.
Level 2 5–8 marks	• Sentence demarcation is largely accurate. • Meaning is largely supported with a range of punctuation. • Some variety of sentence forms is used.	• Standard English is sometimes used, with some inaccuracies in agreement. • Vocabulary choices are varied. • Less common words are often accurately spelled.
Level 1 1–4 marks	• Sentence demarcation is infrequent. • There is limited evidence of deliberate punctuation. • A limited range of sentence forms is used.	• There is limited use of Standard English, with frequent inaccuracies in agreement. • Common words are accurately spelled. • Vocabulary choices are straightforward.
Level 0 0 marks	Poor spelling, punctuation and grammar prevent meaning or understanding.	

I would award the answer .... out of 16 marks because ....

....

....

....

....

Improve the answer

1 A student has written the opening of their response to the following question. Use the hints below to write an improved version.

---

05 Describe an occasion when you could not believe your eyes.

Focus on the thoughts and feelings you had at that time.

(24 marks for content and organisation
16 marks for technical accuracy)
[40 marks]

Had a go

My mum and dad and me went on holiday to lanzarote. My big brother Liam stayed at home to look after the house. When we opened the front door and went inside I could'nt beleive my eyes. All his friends had come round and had a party. The house was a really big mess.

> **Hints**
>
> In every paragraph of your narrative writing, you need to think about the following:
> - the order in which you will sequence your ideas
> - developing your ideas to tell the story clearly and vividly
> - selecting a variety of vocabulary for effect
> - using a range of sentence forms for effect
> - accurate spelling, punctuation and grammar.

....
....
....
....
....
....
....
....
....
....
....
....
....
....
....

Source C

How the birth of the iPhone changed the world forever

The Independent, Monday 26 June 2017

It has taken just 10 years for a five-inch screen to take over almost every aspect of our lives, writes Adrian Weckler

It controls us. Look around any bus, restaurant or public space. Look into any sitting room, or through the windows of stopped cars at traffic lights. Anytime, anywhere - almost everyone is now looking down at a small, five-inch screen.

We stare and stare, the occasional grin or grimace thrown in.

5 The touchscreen gizmo that the late Steve Jobs introduced 10 years ago is now our phone, computer, camera, social life, TV, radio and news service all squished into one device.

It is now hard to function in basic daily life without an iPhone or one of the devices made in its image. Schools and parents' groups now communicate information over (smartphone-only) Whatsapp. Grandparents increasingly depend on Facebook to keep in touch with what relatives are doing. Airlines and travel companies are starting to emphasise phone boarding passes rather than paper ones.

10 Little wonder that survey after survey shows the smartphone as the only indispensable item in our daily routine.

Is this a step forward in civilisation, or the gateway to a dystopian future?

Those complaining about modern ways are often characterised as cranky, middle-aged luddites[1].

"Why can't people chat to one another as they used to in the old days?" they tell radio shows and each other in doctors' waiting rooms. "The smartphone is killing human interaction."

15 Shy, isolated or lonely people may not see it this way. For them, the iPhone has been transformational.

They can now talk to people without many of the usual stigmas and pressures.

As phone networks and broadband services gradually improve, they can access a wider range of news and services without having to travel miles.

They can now feel part of the same society they felt excluded from before.

20 On the other hand, a small screen dictating everything from our language and physical looks to our political opinions has arguably given rise to new forms of narcissism, group-think and social pressure. In a world where photos are effectively the new text, image is more important than ever.

None of this is why Apple invented the iPhone in the first place. It did it to make money. And it has succeeded beyond its wildest dreams.

25 Conservatively, Apple has made over €150bn in profit from the gadget to date, probably the biggest return from any single invention in history in such a short timeframe.

Along its 10-year journey, the iPhone has killed as many industries as it has given birth to.

It's not easy to find a shop selling alarm clocks or home stereos anymore. The compact camera business, for obvious reasons, has collapsed.

30 CDs, already endangered in 2007, are dead too. DVDs are just about to expire, but not because of people watching on PCs. It is the larger screens on phones that is sustaining the huge growth in video streaming.

The iPhone is the single most influential product of the last decade. It could well remain the single most influential for the next.

Glossary:

luddites[1] – English members of organised groups of 19th century craftsmen who opposed the introduction of textile machinery that was displacing them in the midst of the industrial revolution

Source D

In this magazine article, published in 1878, the writer describes one of the very first public demonstrations of an exciting new invention: the telephone.

A Scientific Wonder

On Wednesday last a demonstration of the practical application of the uses of the newly-invented instrument for conveying[1] the human voice, which is known as the telephone, was given at 115, Cannon Street, E.C. The apparatus employed on this occasion may be likened to a small writing desk, having in front of the telephonic operator an electric bell, which can be sounded by the correspondent at the other extremity of the telegraphic wires; there is
5   also a stud which, when pressed, sounds a second electric bell on the distant correspondent's instrument, to call his attention to the impending message. On both sides of the desk are funnel-shaped wooden instruments, the wider end of one of which is applied to the mouth when sending a message, and the other to the ear when receiving one. The smaller end of each instrument is continued into a wire, which is in direct communication with the similar apparatus at which the distant correspondent sits.

10   To transmit a verbal message by the telephone, the sender first touches the electric stud, which causes the bell to sound at the other end of the wire. This may be a few hundred yards or miles distant. Placing one of the instruments to the mouth, the message is spoken, and is received by the distant listener, who has his instrument applied to his ear; and his reply is conveyed back and received in a similar manner.

Contrary to the general belief, the telephone does not convey, so to speak, the actual voice or sound. In the telephone
15   the vibrations of sound interrupt an electric current, and at the other end that interrupted current reproduces the vibrations, and consequently re-creates the sound.

The demonstrations' were perfectly successful: conversation was easily maintained with a distant operator in some other part of the city; the very tones and inflexions[2] of the voice were exactly reproduced; an angry or affectionate message could be sent with appropriate emphasis; and one or two of the ladies present indulged in mild flirtations
20   with the unseen correspondent, sending out soft suspirations[3], and receiving vigorous osculations[4] in return.

The utility and convenience of such an invention are obvious. Instead of sending a telegraphic message[5], requiring time to write, and a skilled operator to transmit, one has but to whisper into the telephone, which, like a speaking tube practically unlimited in length, will convey the message to its required destination. That the telephone will come into general use there is not the slightest doubt. At present it is in its infancy; but the company established by
25   Professor Bell is already engaged in supplying instruments.

The success of the telephone in conveying messages great distances was shown in the experiments recently performed before Her Majesty at Osborne, when a conversation was carried on between London and the Isle of Wight, and vocal and instrumental music was transmitted with success.

Glossary:

conveying[1] – transporting, delivering

inflexions[2] – changes of pitch in a voice

suspirations[3] – sighs

osculations[4] – kisses

telegraphic message[5] – a message sent by telegram using Morse code; the most common form of long distance communication before the invention of the telephone

Source E

Having a baby will simplify your life

The Guardian, Sunday 22 June 2014

Lauren Laverne

Want to be more efficient, motivated
and assertive? Don't bother getting a
life coach – just have a baby

People talk about having children as if it's complicated. Nothing could be further from the truth. It's simple. Simple in the same way that rolling a large boulder up an enormous hill is simple: hard, but simple. Learning the difference between the two has been one of the most useful gifts parenthood has given me, along with the ability to nap anywhere, sometimes accidentally.

5   The truth is that a baby is a fantastic life-simplifying device. It will tell you what to do, all the time. Dealing with the entry and exit points of its food will take up 96% of your day. You will spend the remaining 4% figuring out how to make money to pay for food and nappies. At work you will become more motivated, assertive and efficient via a mixture of desperation, exhaustion and a distorted perspective on what you can achieve.

You made a human!

10   This fact will explode the boundaries of what you believed possible. You'll become fearlessly, selfishly public-spirited, determined to make the world better in order to protect this mysterious being.

Time management will not be a problem. You won't need an alarm. I got up no later than 5.45am for six years. Things I was woken by included screaming, nasal probing, a tooth spat into my hand, the words "Smell this" and the awareness of a tiny, silent, fully costumed Lord Voldemort standing watchfully at the foot of my bed. You won't need a diary. You're 15   not going anywhere. If you do, sheer anticipation of the strange event will render the date unforgettable. In the early weeks, a trip to Asda will warrant the fanfare and pageantry of a royal wedding conducted atop Mount Kilimanjaro.

You will declutter. Lack of time will cause draining "friends" and engagements to evaporate from your life. The idea of owning clothing beyond loungewear that tumble dries will be anathema, which is fine because you will also be freed from the desire to be cool and to travel.

20   When I had two tiny children and three large jobs, I began to fantasise about a time when I would never, ever have to go anywhere or do anything again. This is why parents seem so boring to their teenage children, then surprise them later by doing exciting things: they just need a *massive* rest first. As for keeping up with the latest trends, you won't, and you won't care.

You will live in the moment, not because you're too busy to do otherwise, but because every day will show you how 25   shockingly brief, hilarious, miraculous and precious ordinary family life is. You will get greedy for it, and – frankly – nothing else will do… that's if you're lucky. I hope you are.

Source F

This is an extract from Chapter 1 of *The Terrible Sights of London*, by Thomas Archer. It was written in 1870 as an investigation into the social and economic lives of the poor in London.

The Infant Orphan Asylum at Wanstead

The infant orphan asylum at Wanstead unites the care of children of the earliest age with the functions of a training-school and home. Some baby orphans have been admitted there at the age of six-weeks; and both boys and girls are retained until they are fifteen years old. Six hundred inmates are now receiving the benefits of this most useful charity, many of them the orphan children of clergymen, officers in the army and navy, doctors, lawyers, merchants, master tradesmen,
5   engineers, builders, and contractors.

Well may the committee ask that the institution may be its own advertisement, and invite public inspection by visitors on any Monday or Thursday. I wish I could convey to any eyes that may read these lines the brightness shining through tears that the sight of that great assembly of little souls will occasion; I wish I could hope to make these pages a thousandth part so interesting in their behalf as the sound of their ringing voices must be to every sympathetic tender heart. Then
10   there would be no fear, even though more than nine-tenths of the yearly resources of the charity are derived from voluntary contributions; and the amount of stated annual subscriptions is by no means equivalent to the outlay. They live almost from hand to mouth, these little ones tiny creatures, lying in their little cribs or stretching out their chubby arms to the great British public, – and a great thrill runs through your heart as you give some fair young cherub a finger to grasp in its soft satin-skinned hand. When you get that finger back again, let it join your thumb in clasping a pen to write a
15   cheque, or in taking from your purse a sovereign, a bank-note, representing whatever sum you are prompted to give in the name of Love. Two thousand three hundred and eighty-four little ones have entered that nursery, since the asylum was instituted forty-three years ago. None of them have been more than seven years old, most of them were really infants, and grew up to learn all that is taught there in the schools, of which the Government inspector says:

'I am glad to be able to express my complete satisfaction with the state of all the schools, which, in every respect,
20   seem to be doing very well, and are taught with care and success by their several teachers and assistants.

'The discipline in all the schools is excellent; the Scripture knowledge is also excellent.

'The musical education of the girls is exceedingly satisfactory, and, in common with all the rest of their education, highly creditable to their teachers. The system of teaching French continues to be very successful and valuable in its results.'

The success of numbers of those who, having left that sheltering roof, are now making their own way in the world, is a
25   pretty good proof of the value of their training; and, were it known, might commend the cause of the asylum, which is in great need of regular subscribers to its funds. For the cost is great: the cost of an efficient staff for cooking and preparing the 13,000 meals a-week, and washing the 10,000 articles that represent the laundry-work, to say nothing of the nursing and all the other duties that belong to such a grand baby-show as can be seen in no other country in the world.

Complete the question

1 There are several parts missing from this exam question. Use Source C on page 40 and the answers the student has selected below to complete the question.

01 Read again the first part of **Source C**, from **lines** .... to ....

Choose .... statements below which are ....

- Shade the boxes of the ones that you think are ....
- Choose a maximum of .... statements.

[4 marks]

Nailed it!

A	Smartphones are used by older people as well as younger people.	☒
B	Smartphones have replaced lots of other devices.	☒
C	Smartphones are expensive to buy.	☐
D	Smartphone applications are used by a wide range of people and organisations to communicate and share information.	☒
E	Many schools have banned their students from using smartphones.	☐
F	Surveys show that we think we could not live without our smartphones.	☒
G	Older people find it difficult to use smartphones.	☐
H	Smartphones have made our lives much more difficult in some ways.	☐

You need to look for facts to answer this question. Just because someone's opinion is argued convincingly, it doesn't mean it is a fact.

2 There are several parts missing from this exam question. Use Source C on page 40 and the answers the student has selected below to complete the question.

01 Read again the middle part of **Source C**, from **lines** .... to ....

Choose .... statements below which are ....

- Shade the boxes of the ones that you think are ....
- Choose a maximum of .... statements.

[4 marks]

Nailed it!

A	Some people worry that smartphones have changed the way we communicate.	☒
B	Everyone in a doctor's waiting room is looking at their smartphone.	☐
C	The smartphone has changed some people's lives.	☒
D	Smartphones have made our lives much more difficult in some ways.	☐
E	Smartphones have made us more selfish.	☐
F	The smartphone has made us more concerned about our appearance and what people think of us.	☒
G	The iPhone was invented in order to make money.	☒
H	Shy people prefer to travel long distances rather than use a smartphone.	☐

Mark the answer

1 Use the marking instructions below to decide how many marks you would award this
student's answer.

---

01 Read again **Source C**, from **lines 25 to 32**.

Choose **four** statements below which are TRUE.

I always work out roughly how long I should
spend on each question, and then stick to it!

- Shade the boxes of the ones that you think are true.

- Choose a maximum of four statements.

[4 marks]

A   Apple was the first place that invented the iPhone.   ⬭

B   The iPhone may be the most profitable invention ever.   ▨

C   Alarm clocks and home stereos have become much more expensive.   ▨

D   Lots of companies have gone out of business because of the smartphone.   ⬭

E   Very few people buy CDs anymore.   ⬭

F   Some phones have larger screens than some computers.   ▨

G   The iPhone will continue to change the way we live in the future.   ▨

H   Apple may stop making smartphones in the future.   ⬭

Marking instructions
• Identify and interpret explicit and implicit information and ideas.
Give 1 mark for each correct statement which is true.

I would award the answer .... out of 4 marks because ....

....

....

....

....

....

....

....

....

Complete the question

1 Complete the question by adding **eight** statements for A to H below. Use Source E on page 42 and the hints below to help. Make sure four statements are correct.

01 Read again the first part of **Source E**, from **lines 1 to 11**.

Choose **four** statements below which are TRUE.

- Shade the boxes of the ones that you think are true.
- Choose a maximum of four statements. [4 marks]

> **Hints**
> - You need to infer information from the Source to answer these kinds of questions.
> - The information may not be clearly stated in the Source so you might have to 'read between the lines' to work out the answers.

A .... ▨

....

B .... ▨

....

C .... ◻

....

D .... ▨

....

E .... ▨

....

F .... ◻

....

G .... ◻

....

H .... ◻

....

Find the answer

1 Which of the three paragraphs below would you include in your answer to the following question? Explain your choice. Then, explain why you would **not** include the other two paragraphs.

---

02 You need to refer to **Source C** and **Source D** for this question.

Use details from **both** Sources. Write a summary of the differences between the two inventions. **[8 marks]**

> Remember to read the question carefully. What are you being asked to compare? Are you being asked to identify similarities or differences?

Paragraph A — You get the impression from Source D that the telephone was an amazing invention when it was first invented. The writer describes it using very positive language and says he has "not the slightest doubt" that everyone will want one and use it all the time. In the same way, the writer of Source C shows what an amazing invention the smartphone was. It's used by "everyone" for a whole range of things. He describes it as "our phone, computer, camera, social life, TV, radio and news service all squished into one device." Both writers show that these inventions are or will be really popular.

Paragraph B — In Source C, the writer explains that the smartphone has changed our lives in the ten years since it was first invented. He gives examples to show how we take it everywhere and use it in lots of different ways. In Source D, however, the writer is writing about a new invention that not many people would know about and he has to explain how it works. He does think, though, that it will definitely "come into general use" and so predicts how popular it will be. So one text is about a new invention that is not yet very well known, and the other text is about a ten year old invention that everyone knows about and uses.

Paragraph C — Source C tells you how popular the smartphone is with all kinds of people because children and teenagers use it all the time, grandparents use it to keep in touch with their grandchildren, parents use it to check what their children are doing and when they will be home, and lots of businesses use it for making deals and talking to each other. When the telephone was first invented though it was only popular with people who were doing demonstrations and with Queen Victoria so not many people used it. The biggest difference between the two inventions is how popular they are.

I would include paragraph .... because ....

....

....

....

I would not include paragraphs .... or .... because ....

....

....

....

Mark the answer

1 Draw lines to connect each of the marker's comments to a relevant part (or parts) of this student's answer. One has been done for you.

> **02** You need to refer to **Source C** and **Source D** for this question.
>
> Use details from **both** Sources. Write a summary of the differences between the two inventions. **[8 marks]**
>
> Both texts give a clear impression of what each invention looks like, but the descriptions look very, very different. The only description of a smartphone in Source C is when the writer talks about a "small, five-inch screen", which most people would know means a smartphone. In Source D, though, the writer has to give a very long description of the telephone because no one would know what one looked like back then. He says the telephone "may be likened to a small writing desk, having in front of the telephonic operator an electric bell, which can be sounded by the correspondent at the other extremity of the telegraphic wires". You get the impression of a very big machine that is much bigger than a smartphone.

Relevant, focused evidence.

Relevant but overlong and unfocused evidence.

Clear inferences drawn from both texts. (× 2)

A clear difference between the texts identified.

2 Now use the mark scheme below to decide how many marks you would award the answer.

Level	Skills descriptors
Level 4 7–8 marks	Response demonstrates insightful synthesis and interpretation of both texts: • insightful inferences are drawn from both texts • gives a carefully selected range of relevant, focused evidence from both texts • a range of insightful differences between texts are identified.
Level 3 5–6 marks	Response demonstrates clear synthesis and interpretation of both texts: • clear inferences are drawn from both texts • gives a range of relevant, focused textual evidence from both texts • clear differences between texts are identified.
Level 2 3–4 marks	Response demonstrates some interpretation of one or both texts: • some inference is drawn from one or both texts • textual evidence from one or both texts is relevant and focused • significant differences between texts are identified.
Level 1 1–2 marks	Response demonstrates some awareness of one or both texts: • understanding is largely literal rather than inferential • textual evidence from one or both texts is largely relevant • simple differences between texts are identified.
Level 0 No marks	No differences identified. No rewardable response.

I would award the answer .... out of 8 marks because ....

....

....

....

Connect the comments

1 Three students have written answers to the following question. Draw lines to connect the marker's comments to the relevant extracts.

02 You need to refer to **Source C** and **Source D** for this question.

Use details from **both** Sources. Write a summary of the differences between the two inventions. **[8 marks]**

> **Hint**
> • The best answers give a clear judgement on the success of the writers' choices and their effects.

Extract A

The biggest difference between the two inventions is probably what they can do. In Source C, the writer sums up how many different functions and apps a smartphone has. He says it is a "phone, computer, camera, social life, TV, radio and news service all squished into one device." This suggests how useful a smartphone is in lots of different ways. The telephone in Source D, however, can only do one thing: "conveying the human voice".

The response demonstrates an interpretation of only one text, making some inference supported with relevant, focused evidence.

Extract B

In Source D, the writer tries to show how useful a telephone is. He explains that it can be used for "conveying messages", which it does "perfectly", but also "vocal and instrumental music" can be "transmitted with success". This shows what a useful and amazing invention this was at the time that it was invented.

The response shows some synthesis and interpretation of each text and draws some inference from both, supported with relevant evidence.

Extract C

In Source C, you get the impression that the smartphone is useful for lots of different things but that it has a negative side. For example, the writer lists all the things it can do: "computer, camera, social life, TV, radio and news service" but also highlights how it has taken over our lives: "It controls us" and some people think it is "killing human interaction". However, in Source D the writer gives only the positive things about the telephone. He says, "The utility and convenience of such an invention are obvious", suggesting a more naïve attitude towards technology.

The response shows clear synthesis of perceptive inferences from both texts, identifying a significant difference, supported with a range of relevant evidence.

Build the answer

1 Which of the sentences below could you use in a response to this question? Tick them.

02   You need to refer to **Source E** and **Source F** for this question.

Use details from **both** Sources. Write a summary of the differences between being a parent and
running an orphanage.   **[8 marks]**

> In this type of question,
> you don't need to analyse
> or comment on the writers'
> choices. You just need to
> compare the information
> given in the two sources and
> draw some inference from it.

☐ **A**   In Source E the writer talks about having a baby and looking after "two tiny children".

☐ **B**   One of the most obvious differences between being a parent and running an orphanage shown in the two Sources is the number of children you have to look after.

☐ **C**   In Source F the writer points out in the first paragraph the huge number of children that are looked after at the orphanage: "Six hundred inmates are now receiving the benefits of this most useful charity."

☐ **D**   The writer uses alliteration to emphasise how small and vulnerable her children were.

☐ **E**   The writer of Source F has a very positive attitude to children whereas the writer of Source E gives both the positive and negative sides.

☐ **F**   Describing the orphans as "inmates" suggests that the orphanage is like a prison, although this may not have been what the writer wanted to suggest.

☐ **G**   This could suggest that running an orphanage would take a lot more work, and a lot more people to do the work, than looking after just two children.

☐ **H**   Source F also gives a lot of information about everything that the orphans are taught, and how well they are taught it.

2 Look at the sentences you have **not** ticked. Explain why you would **not** include each one
in your response.

....

....

....

....

....

3 Look again at the sentences you have ticked. Which order (A, B, C etc.) would you put them in
to build an effective response to the question?

....

Improve the answer

1 Improve the paragraph below. Use the hints to make sure your paragraph achieves the highest possible mark. Continue on a second sheet of paper if needed.

02 You need to refer to **Source E** and **Source F** for this question.

Use details from **both** Sources. Write a summary of the differences between being a parent and running an orphanage.

[8 marks]

Had a go

Another important difference between running an orphanage and being a parent is the amount of work that has to be done. Only one Source talks about the number of meals that have to be cooked and the number of things that have to be washed. The text about the orphanage gives lots of information about how the children are educated. The other text does not.

> **Hints**
>
> To write an effective synthesis and summary response, you need to do the following:
> - identify a significant similarity or difference in the two texts
> - use evidence from both texts to support your point
> - make clear what can be inferred by comparing the information in the two texts
> - signal that you are making a comparison by using adverbials or conjunctions, for example 'however', 'whereas', 'similarly'.

Complete the answer

1 Complete the student's answer to achieve the highest possible mark.

02 You need to refer to **Source E** and **Source F** for this question.

Use details from **both** Sources. Write a summary of the differences between being a parent and running an orphanage.

[8 marks]

I tackle compare questions like this by finding pairs – matching similar or related information in the two texts. For example, if the writer of one text suggests that looking after children is expensive, I would try to find something the writer of the other text suggests about the cost of looking after children.

Although both writers comment on the need for money to look after children

The Sources suggest different ways to cope with the hard work of looking after children.

Source F suggests that the main achievement of the orphanage is educating the children and preparing them

Complete the question

1 There are several parts missing from this exam question. Use Source D on page 41 and the extracts from the three student responses below to complete the question.

03 You now need to refer **only** to **Source D**, from lines .... to ....

How does the writer use language to ....? **[12 marks]**

Nailed it!

Student A
In the first sentence of the first paragraph of the Source the writer explains that this new invention is for "conveying the human voice". This short, simple explanation gives the reader a basic understanding of the telephone.

Student B
The writer uses purposeful language choices to describe the appearance of this new invention. He compares it to "a small writing desk" and describes parts as "funnel-shaped" so that the reader can imagine things they already know and then imagine the telephone.

Student C
In the final paragraph of this part of the Source, the writer uses simple, scientific language to explain how the telephone works, for example, "the vibrations of sound interrupt an electric current". Using these simple terms helps the reader to understand how it works.

2 There are several parts missing from this exam question. Use Source D on page 41 and the extracts from the three student responses below to complete the question.

03 You now need to refer **only** to **Source D**, from lines .... to ....

How does the writer use language to make ....

....? **[12 marks]**

> You should always read the question twice and check whether you are being asked to write about the whole Source or just one part of it.

Nailed it!

Student A
At the start of this part of the Source, the writer highlights all the different benefits of the telephone. He explains them all, using a series of clauses separated with semi-colons, which helps to emphasise just how many benefits there are. For example, "conversation" can be "easily maintained" and tone of voice is "exactly reproduced". This positive language helps to persuade the reader of the telephone's benefits.

Student B
The writer also shows the different kinds of messages that can be delivered using a telephone. One way he does this is by using contrasting adjectives: "an angry or affectionate message could be sent", which shows that the emotion in the messages can easily be heard. He even describes "mild flirtations", humorously showing that even romantic conversations can be had over the telephone!

Student C
Throughout this part of the Source, the writer repeatedly emphasises how well the telephone does its job and how it will make communication easier. For example, when the writer describes the demonstration that was performed for Her Majesty, he repeats the word "success" twice in the same paragraph, which emphasises how reliable the telephone is.

Find the answer

1 Which of the three points below would you include in your answer to the following question? Explain your choice. Then, explain why you would **not** include the other two points.

---

03   You now need to refer **only** to Source D, from **lines 1 to 16**.

How does the writer use language to explain this new invention to the reader?   **[12 marks]**

> I always have to check that I'm answering the question. It's easy to forget what the question is actually asking you to do – you can end up just describing what the Source is about!

Point A
: The writer carefully describes the appearance of the telephone. He describes all the different parts of the phone in detail. For example, he explains the shape of the instrument you hold up to your ear, describing it as "funnel-shaped" and "wooden". This helps the reader to imagine using the phone and makes it easier to understand how it works.

Point B
: The writer uses lots of descriptive language to explain how the telephone works. For example, he describes what the telephone looks like, he describes how to use it and he describes how it works. This all helps to explain this new invention to the reader.

Point C
: The writer describes how well the telephone works, explaining that the demonstrations were "perfectly successful", which might persuade the reader to want to buy and use a telephone now they know how to.

I would include point   because
....

I would not include points   or   because
....

....

---

2 A different student has written three points in response to the same question. Which point would you **not** include in your answer? Explain your choice.

Point A
: The writer uses comparisons to help the reader understand what this new invention is like. For example, he compares the telephone to "a small writing desk", which readers at this time would have been more able to imagine.

Point B
: The writer uses some technical language to show how the telephone works, saying that "the vibrations of sound interrupt an electric current". This simple scientific language suggests how clever the invention is to use this method to send the sound of the human voice through wires.

Point C
: The telephone described in the Source is very different to a modern telephone. For example, you make the other person's phone ring by pressing "the electric stud". This would have needed explaining to the reader at this time because they probably would never have seen this new invention.

I would not include point   because
....

....

....

Mark the answer

1 Draw lines to connect each of the marker's comments to a relevant part of this student's answer.
One has been done for you.

03   You now need to refer **only** to **Source D**, from **lines 17 to 28**.

How does the writer use language to make you, the reader, understand the benefits of the telephone?   **[12 marks]**

The writer shows the benefits of the telephone by

saying it is like a speaking tube "practically unlimited

in length", which suggests that the power of the

telephone is unlimited because it can deliver messages

anywhere. The writer also describes the telephone

as being "in its infancy", which suggests that the

telephone is like a child that will grow and become

much stronger. Beginning this sentence with the words

"At present" suggests that this might happen soon.

> Relevant evidence is used to support comments.

> A limited comment on language choice with little explanation or analysis.

> Comment on sentence form is limited but valid.

> A valid, developed comment on language choice, focused on its effect.

> An opportunity to use subject terminology is missed.

2 Now use the mark scheme below to decide how many marks you would award the answer.

Level	Skills descriptors
Level 4 10–12 marks	Response demonstrates a developed and insightful appreciation of the writer's use of language: • clear and detailed analysis of the effect of the writer's language choices • a carefully selected range of relevant, focused textual evidence • a range of subject terminology to achieve clarity and precision.
Level 3 7–9 marks	Response demonstrates clear appreciation of the writer's use of language: • clear comments on the effect of the writer's language choices • a range of relevant, focused textual evidence • a range of subject terminology to achieve clarity.
Level 2 4–6 marks	Response demonstrates some appreciation of the writer's use of language: • some comments on the effect of the writer's language choices • relevant and focused textual evidence • largely accurate subject terminology.
Level 1 1–3 marks	Response demonstrates some awareness of the writer's use of language: • straightforward comments on the effect of the writer's language choices • largely relevant textual evidence • some use of subject terminology, with inconsistent accuracy.
Level 0 No marks	No comments made on the writer's use of language. No rewardable response.

I would award the answer   out of 12 marks because

....

....

....

Connect the comments

1 Three students have written answers to the following question. Draw lines to connect each of the marker's comments to the relevant extract.

03 You now need to refer **only** to **Source D**, from **lines 17 to 28**.

How does the writer use language to make you, the reader, understand the benefits of the telephone? **[12 marks]**

I always have to remind myself that long answers are not always better answers!

Extract A

Throughout the Source the writer uses positive adverbials to highlight the benefits of the telephone. The demonstration was "perfectly successful", conversations were "easily maintained" and the voices were "exactly reproduced", emphasising to the reader the fact that the telephone is simple to use and completely reliable.

The response shows some awareness of the writer's use of language and makes a straightforward comment on its effect, supported with relevant evidence. However, the response also summarises details from the Source without making any further comment on the writer's use of language.

Extract B

The writer compares the telephone with a telegraphic message to show how much better it is. The writer uses the phrases "time to write" and "a skilled operator" to show how complicated it is to send a telegraphic message. In contrast, the writer uses the verb "whisper" to show how easy it is to send a message using the telephone.

The response shows some appreciation of a range of the writer's language choices, selecting relevant focused evidence and accurately using subject terminology to comment on its effect. Comments could be developed to analyse the writer's use of language in more detail.

Extract C

The writer describes the way the telephone worked in the demonstration as "perfectly successful", which shows that the telephone works well and is a good invention. It also tells you how well it worked because it says the voices were clear and the two people on the phone could hear what the other person was saying and they could understand how the other person was feeling, which shows how clear their voices were and how well the telephone works.

This response shows a clear and developed appreciation of the writer's language choices, analysing their effect in detail, supported with a range of relevant focused evidence and accurate subject terminology.

Build the answer

1 Look at the question below and Source F on page 43. Which sentences would you use in your response? Tick them.

03 You now need to refer **only** to **Source F**, from **lines 1 to 18**.

How does the writer use language to make you, the reader, feel you would like to help the orphans? **[12 marks]**

☐ **A** In this part of the Source, the writer gives the reader the impression that the children in the orphanage are like angels but also very vulnerable.

☐ **B** The writer presents the orphans in a really positive way.

☐ **C** The writer uses lots of descriptive words to persuade the reader to give money to the orphanage.

☐ **D** The writer uses alliteration to describe an orphan's "soft satin-skinned hand", which makes it sound very fragile, as though the child can easily be hurt and needs to be protected.

☐ **E** The writer asks the reader to imagine meeting one of the babies and the "great thrill" that will run "through your heart" when you do. The noun "thrill" and the verb "runs" suggest how strongly you would feel sympathy and affection for the child.

☐ **F** The writer highlights how small and vulnerable the orphans are, using the adjectives "tiny" and "little" to suggest that they need the reader's help.

☐ **G** The overall impression the writer gives in this part of the Source is of a beautiful baby that needs your affection and your money.

2 Look at the sentences you have **not** ticked. Explain why you would **not** include each one in your response.

....
....
....
....

3 Look again at the sentences you have ticked. Which order (A, B, C etc.) would you put them in to build an effective response to the question?

....

Re-order the answer

1 The paragraphs below are taken from a student's response to the following question.
Rearrange the paragraphs into the most logical order by numbering them from 1 to 4.

03 You now need to refer **only** to **Source F**, from **lines 1 to 18**.

How does the writer use language to make you, the reader, feel you would like to help the orphans? **[12 marks]**

> I always plan my answer by spending a minute noting down my ideas and putting them in the best order.

☐ Furthermore, the writer suggests how sorry you should feel for them. He says that the orphans would be interesting to "every sympathetic tender heart", using positive language choices to flatter the reader and make them want to feel sorry for the orphans and to help them. It makes you feel that if you are not interested and do not want to help them, you are different to everyone else and you are cruel.

☐ The writer begins the Source by writing about the kinds of children at the orphanage. He uses a long list to show all the different types of family the orphans come from, including "clergymen, officers in the army... doctors, lawyers". This suggests they come from rich parents whom they have now lost. This might make the reader feel sorry for them.

☐ The writer tries to appeal to the reader by describing the orphans in detail. He focuses on their "ringing voices", their "chubby arms" and their "soft satin-skinned hand". The word "ringing" suggests their voices make a musical noise, while their "soft satin" skin makes them sound precious but delicate. These adjectives are used to make the orphans sound as appealing as possible, and to make the reader feel sorry for them.

☐ At the end of this part of the Source, the writer again emphasises the number of different children the orphanage has helped using a statistic, explaining that "Two thousand three hundred and eighty-four little ones have entered that nursery" since it began. This emphasises how much good work the orphanage does and how much it needs your help.

2 Now, explain your choice.

> You can organise your answer by writing about each part, or each different idea in the Source in turn.

....

....

....

....

....

Complete the answer

1 Complete the student's answer to achieve the highest possible mark.

03 You now need to refer **only** to **Source F**, from **lines 19 to 28**.

How does the writer use language to make you, the reader, feel you would like to make a donation to the orphanage?

[12 marks]

> Highlight the language choices you want to comment on in the Source. Then you'll be able to see all the choices you want to comment on and find them much more quickly when you come to write your response.

The writer quotes the Government Inspector focusing on ....

....

....

....

The writer describes the orphanage as "a grand baby-show" to suggest that ....

....

....

....

....

The writer uses statistics to highlight how much work the orphanage does to help the ....

children, for example: ....

....

....

....

....

The writer positions "For the cost is great" at the start of a sentence to ....

....

....

....

....

Find the answer

1 Which of the three points below would you **not** include in your answer to the following question? Explain your choice. Then, explain why you would include the other two points.

04   For this question, you need to refer to the **whole of Source C**, together with **Source D**.

Compare how the two writers convey their different attitudes to technology.

In your answer, you could:

- compare their different attitudes
- compare the methods they use to convey their attitudes
- support your ideas with references to both texts.

> Remember to read the question carefully and make sure your answer concentrates on the writers' attitudes.

[16 marks]

A   The writer of Source D uses some humour in the article. He describes how two ladies at the demonstration "indulged in mild flirtations" and were giving out "suspirations", which means sighs, and getting "osculations", which means kisses, down the telephone. This helps to make the article interesting. Source C, on the other hand, does not use any humour. It is quite negative and concentrates on how smartphones are controlling us and shutting down lots of businesses.

B   Both texts emphasise the popularity of the technology they are writing about, but in different ways. In Source C the writer highlights how "everyone" uses a smartphone, "looking down" at it, suggesting that they are in their own world and ignoring everyone and everything else. In Source D, however, the writer thinks that the telephone will become a very popular thing in the future because of its "utility and convenience". He highlights how good it is for communicating with other people, describing how well it can convey "an angry or affectionate message" and even "osculations".

C   The writers of the two Sources have very different attitudes to technology. One seems to be worried or even frightened about it, whereas the other welcomes it. In Source C, the writer seems unsure whether the smartphone is "a step forward" or "the gateway to a dystopian future" suggesting that he thinks technology may lead human beings to misery and disaster. In Source D, however, the writer can see nothing bad about the telephone. He thinks it is "A Scientific Wonder", which suggests that he admires its inventor and thinks science and technology should be admired.

I would not include point   because ....

....

....

I would include points   and   because ....

....

....

....

....

Mark the answer

1 Draw lines to connect each of the marker's comments to a relevant part (or parts) of this student's answer. One has been done for you.

04 For this question, you need to refer to the **whole of Source C**, together with **Source D**.

Compare how the two writers convey their different attitudes to technology.

In your answer, you could:

- compare their different attitudes
- compare the methods they use to convey their attitudes
- support your ideas with references to both texts.

[16 marks]

The writers show different attitudes to the ways in which technology can change our lives, expressed in similar ways. In Source D, instead of explaining how the telephone will change people's lives, he says "The utility and convenience … are obvious." The short, simple statement adds emphasis to his point, and the word "obvious" suggests that there is no need to explain the benefits of technology. In Source C, however, the writer seems concerned about the ways the smartphone has changed our lives. For example, in the first sentence of the Source, he says "It controls us." This negative view, like the view in Source D, is given in a short, emphatic sentence that makes it sound like an unarguable fact.

> A clear comparison of the writers' attitudes.

> Relevant, focused evidence. (× 2)

> A clear explanation of the writers' choices. (× 2)

> A clear understanding of the different attitudes.

2 Now use the mark scheme below to decide how many marks you would award the answer.

Level	Skills descriptors
Level 4 13–16 marks	Response demonstrates insightful comparison of the writers' ideas and perspectives: • clear and detailed analysis of the writers' choices • a carefully selected range of relevant, focused textual evidence from both texts • a developed and considered understanding of the different ideas and perspectives in both texts.
Level 3 9–12 marks	Response demonstrates clear comparison of the writers' ideas and perspectives: • clear explanation on the writers' choices • a range of relevant, focused textual evidence from both texts • a clear understanding of the different ideas and perspectives in both texts.
Level 2 5–8 marks	Response demonstrates limited comparison of the writers' ideas and perspectives: • some comments on the writers' choices • relevant and focused textual evidence from one or both texts • awareness of a range of different ideas and perspectives.
Level 1 1–4 marks	Response demonstrates simple cross-referencing of the writers' ideas and perspectives: • straightforward comments on the writers' choices • largely relevant textual evidence • some awareness of ideas and/or perspectives.
Level 0 No marks	No comments made on the differences. No rewardable response.

I would award the answer   out of 16 marks because

....

....

....

Connect the comments

1 Three students have written answers to the following question. Draw lines to connect each of the marker's comments to the relevant extract.

04 For this question, you need to refer to the **whole of Source C**, together with **Source D**.

Compare how the two writers convey their different attitudes to technology.

In your answer, you could:

- compare their different attitudes
- compare the methods they use to convey their attitudes
- support your ideas with references to both texts.

[16 marks]

Extract A

Both writers think that technology can be a good thing. For example, the writer of Source D thinks that the telephone is a great invention. He writes about the telephone's success and how it works "perfectly". In Source C, the writer also talks about smartphones being a good thing, although he does have some negatives. He thinks it is a good thing for people who are "shy, isolated or lonely" because they can talk to people without feeling under pressure. So, both writers think that technology can be a good thing.

The response makes a simple comparison of the two Sources but with little reference to the writers' attitudes. Relevant but limited evidence is used to support the comparison.

Extract B

In Source C the writer talks a lot about how much money Apple have made from smartphones. He says they've made 150 billion and he thinks it is the most profitable invention ever. This is because it is so popular and it's the best smartphone and everyone wants one even though it's expensive. In Source D the writer does not say much about money but he does say something about the company that makes them. So, one text is about the money you can make from technology but the other one is not.

The response makes a clear comparison of the writers' attitudes, supported with a range of relevant evidence, but needs to give more attention to commenting on the writers' choices and their effect.

Extract C

Both writers are writing about the impact of technology, but from different points of view. In Source C, the writer compares positive and negative attitudes to smartphones: those who feel it is "killing human interaction" and others who might once have "felt excluded" but now "feel part" of society. This comparison suggests the writer has mixed feelings. The writer of Source D is thinking about the impact the telephone will have in the future. To convince the reader that it will soon be "in general use", he concentrates throughout his article on explaining to the reader how it works "perfectly". One writer is highlighting the impact that technology has had and the other is convincing the reader that it will have an impact.

The response makes a clear comparison of the writers' attitudes and intentions, supported with a detailed analysis of some of the writers' structural choices and their impact on the reader.

Build the answer

1 Look at the question below and Sources E and F on pages 42–43. Which sentences would you use in your response? Tick them.

04　For this question, you need to refer to the **whole of Source E**, together with **Source F**.

Compare how the two writers convey their different attitudes to children.

In your answer, you could:

- compare their different attitudes
- compare the methods they use to convey their attitudes
- support your ideas with references to both texts.

> You can compare how the writers use similar language techniques to show different attitudes.

[16 marks]

☐ A　It implies the child is a ruthless and evil being who will stop at nothing to get what it wants.

☐ B　The writer of Source F makes a positive comparison.

☐ C　She uses a metaphor to compare one of her own children to "Lord Voldemort".

☐ D　He uses a metaphor to compare a baby to a "fair young cherub".

☐ E　This suggests that children are like small, beautiful angels and are pure and perfect in every way.

☐ F　This comparison is used to create humour but it does imply the power that children have over their parents.

☐ G　The government inspector in Source F describes their education as "excellent" and "exceedingly satisfactory", which suggests how well the orphans are looked after.

☐ H　Both writers use metaphors to convey their attitudes to children.

☐ I　On the other hand, the writer of Source E makes a negative comparison.

2 Look at the sentences you have **not** ticked. Explain why you would **not** include each one in your response.

....

....

....

3 Look again at the sentences you have ticked. Which order (A, B, C etc.) would you put them in to build an effective response to the question?

....

Improve the answer

1 Write an improved answer to the question below. Use the hints to make sure your answer achieves the highest possible mark. Continue on a second sheet of paper if needed.

04 For this question, you need to refer to the **whole of Source E**, together with **Source F**.

Compare how the two writers convey their different attitudes to children.

In your answer, you could:
- compare their different attitudes
- compare the methods they use to convey their attitudes
- support your ideas with references to both texts.

[16 marks]

Had a go

The two Sources give different impressions of children. One has a positive attitude but the other uses a negative attitude to create humour. Source F says "The success of numbers of those who [...] are now making their own way in the world". This gives the impression that children should be educated in how to be independent. The writer suggests that the orphanage does this well. Source E gives the impression that preparing children for adult life is not so important. The main thing is to try to enjoy being with them.

> **Hints**
>
> To write an effective comparison of the writers' attitudes, you need to do the following:
> - use evidence from both texts to identify a significant similarity or difference.
> - make comparisons using adverbials or conjunctions (however, whereas, etc.).

....

....

....

....

....

....

....

....

....

....

....

....

....

....

....

....

....

Complete the answer

1 Complete the student's answer to achieve the highest possible mark.

04 For this question, you need to refer to the **whole of Source E**, together with **Source F**.

Compare how the two writers convey their different attitudes to children.

In your answer, you could:

- compare their different attitudes
- compare the methods they use to convey their attitudes
- support your ideas with references to both texts.

[16 marks]

In Source F, the writer's attitude to the children in the orphanage is that they are weak and
helpless and need the reader's support.

....

....

....

....

....

....

Source E gives a very negative impression of children in almost every paragraph.

....

....

....

....

....

....

Although Source E is very negative to begin with, both writers show positive attitudes
to children.

....

....

....

....

....

....

....

Build the answer

1 Which of the ideas below would you use in a plan responding to this exam-style writing task? Tick them.

05 'Computers and phones rule everything we do. We can't think without them, go anywhere without them, or live without them. Technology has taken over our lives.'

Write an article for a broadsheet newspaper in which you explain your point of view on this statement.

(24 marks for content and organisation
16 marks for technical accuracy)
[40 marks]

☐ A   We rely on phones and computers because they are so useful.

☐ B   I like my phone because I like sharing funny videos with my mates.

☐ C   Some people get obsessed with social media, checking it every minute of the day and some of the night too.

☐ D   You never feel lonely or bored because you can always find someone to talk to or something to look at or read.

☐ E   It's some of the older generations that complain we are obsessed with technology because they don't understand how to use it or the benefits it has.

☐ F   One of my granddads is on social media all the time, talking to my cousins in New Zealand. My other grandad says I spend all day staring at my phone and I should go out and get some fresh air!

☐ G   Technology has been taking over our lives for hundreds of years: steam engines, trains, cars, planes, electricity, television, etc.

☐ H   We can't stop progress. Why would we want to stop it if it makes our lives easier and better?

☐ I   The smartphone has replaced the camera, CD player, calendar, clock, etc., all in one tiny box.

2 Look at the ideas you have **not** ticked. Explain why you would **not** include each one in your plan.

....
....
....

3 Look again at the sentences you have ticked. Which order (A, B, C etc.) would you put them in to build an effective response to the question?

....

Find the answer

1 Which of the openings below would you **not** use to begin your answer to this question? Explain your choice. Then, explain why you would include the other two openings.

> **05** 'Computers and phones rule everything we do. We can't think without them, go anywhere without them, or live without them. Technology has taken over our lives.'
>
> Write an article for a broadsheet newspaper in which you explain your point of view on this statement.
>
> (24 marks for content and organisation
> 16 marks for technical accuracy)
> **[40 marks]**

> Remember why you are writing and who you are writing for – your writing needs to suit your purpose and your audience.

> A — Every hour of every day, we rely on technology to help us.

> B — I reckon the mobile phone and computer are the best inventions in the world ever. End of.

> C — Technology is changing faster and faster every day.

I would not use opening   because
....
....
I would use opening   or   because
....
....

2 Which of the openings below would you **not** use to begin your answer to this question? Explain your choice. Then, explain why you would include the other two points.

> A — Sit on a bus or in a café and look around you. Everyone is staring at their phones. No one is talking.

> Your first sentence needs to grab the reader's attention.

> B — Door keys, money, phone. These are the three things we all take when we leave the house, because they all make our lives much easier and safer.

> C — In this article I am going to explain my point of view on technology and why I think it is a good thing.

I would not use opening   because ....
....
....
I would use opening   or   because ....
....
....

Connect the comments

1 Three students have written answers to the following question. Draw lines to connect each of the marker's comments to the relevant extract.

05   'Computers and phones rule everything we do. We can't think without them, go anywhere without them, or live without them. Technology has taken over our lives.'

Write an article for a broadsheet newspaper in which you explain your point of view on this statement.

(24 marks for content and organisation
16 marks for technical accuracy)
[40 marks]

Extract A

I use my phone all the time, I mean 24-7, because it does so many different things I need. I use it in school to talk to my friends and as a calculator in maths and I use it at home to watch videos and go on social media and a whole load of other stuff. My mum says I'm on it too much but she's got a phone though she doesn't really know how to use it properly. My dad's got a tablet but he just looks at the football results and plays games on it.

The response inconsistently explains the writer's point of view using some inappropriately informal language. There are some relevant ideas but they are inconsistently linked.

Extract B

Technology saves lives. Whether it's the equipment in a hospital or the equipment used by the emergency services when they are searching for someone in danger or difficulty, we have come to rely on technology to keep us safe, to make us healthy, and to keep us alive. Technology has taken over our lives because it improves our lives.

The response uses a range of linked ideas to engage the reader, with some vocabulary choices selected for effect. The response explains the writer's point of view using appropriately formal language.

Extract C

Social media would not exist without smartphones and computers. There are some benefits to social media. For example, it is a good way to talk to friends and share pictures and jokes and ideas. However, there are some bad sides to social media too. For example, my little sister is obsessed with it. She checks her page at least once every five minutes and I know she looks at it after she is supposed to be asleep, and she gets upset when people post horrible comments. That is the worst thing about social media. You don't have to be nice. People think they can be cruel, vicious and spiteful and they think it doesn't matter.

The response consistently and effectively explains the writer's point of view using a variety of sentence forms, and a broad range of vocabulary and rhetorical devices, carefully crafted for effect. Ideas are clearly linked and fully developed to engage and influence the reader.

Re-order the answer

1 The sentences below are taken from the introduction of a response to the following question. Rearrange the sentences into the most logical order by numbering them from 1 to 8.

05 'Computers and phones rule everything we do. We can't think without them, go anywhere without them, or live without them. Technology has taken over our lives.'

Write an article for a broadsheet newspaper in which you explain your point of view on this statement.

(24 marks for content and organisation
16 marks for technical accuracy)
[40 marks]

☐ When we stare at our phones, we think we're keeping in touch with friends and family and the world.

☐ Perhaps we should be frightened.

☐ Perhaps we should think twice.

> The best introductions get the reader interested immediately and make them think.

☐ When we ask our virtual personal assistant what the weather will be like today or when that maths homework is due in, we think technology is our friend.

☐ Should we love technology and believe that it can only make our lives better?

☐ Perhaps we should wonder whether technology has only just begun to take over our lives.

☐ Perhaps we should beware.

☐ When we use our computers, we think they're making us better informed or saving us time or helping us work.

Mark the answer

1 Draw lines to connect each of the marker's comments to a relevant part of this student's answer. One has been done for you.

05   'Computers and phones rule everything we do. We can't think without them, go anywhere without them, or live without them. Technology has taken over our lives.'

Write an article for a broadsheet newspaper in which you explain your point of view on this statement.

(24 marks for content and organisation
16 marks for technical accuracy)
[40 marks]

I lost my phone for a day once and I spent
hours and hours looking for it and I couldn't find
it anywhere and I realised how much I use it
and need it and I felt kind of lost without it.
It shows how much we need phones and
technology and how we've got used to having
them and we can't live without them.

> A relevant key point is made based on personal experience but it is not developed.

> Informal language choice is inappropriate for the task.

> Repetitive sentence structure weakens the impact of the writer's ideas.

> Vocabulary is limited, expressing ideas clearly but with little impact.

2 Draw lines to connect each of the marker's comments to a relevant part of this student's answer.

We often think of technology as being something
that is used only by young people, organising
their social lives, talking to their vast group of
friends, sharing photos and videos. However,
technology can help the lonely, the isolated and
the elderly by giving them a direct line to the
rest of the world. A grandmother living on her
own can chat to her grandchildren on the other
side of the world. An elderly man can text his
shopping list to a friendly, helpful neighbour who
can order it online and get it delivered, then
chat to his friend from the old days who lives
hundreds of miles away, or in a different country.
Technology can help us all, young and old.

> A developed key point clearly explains the writer's point of view.

> A range of examples support the writer's point of view.

> The writer's point of view is expressed clearly and precisely through careful vocabulary choices.

> Short sentence form gives emphasis to the writer's point of view.

Build the answer

1 Look at this question and the student's sentences below. Which sentences would you use in the main section of a response to this question? Tick them.

05 'Computers and phones rule everything we do. We can't think without them, go anywhere without them, or live without them. Technology has taken over our lives.'

Write an article for a broadsheet newspaper in which you explain your point of view on this statement.

(24 marks for content and organisation
16 marks for technical accuracy)
[40 marks]

☐ A   I think technology is killing our ability to communicate with each other.

☐ B   People often say that technology helps us communicate more effectively with each other.

☐ C   Sometimes my friends message me on my phone when we are in the same room.

☐ D   My sister messages my mum from her room, asking her to bring her some food or a drink.

☐ E   Amazingly, my mum actually takes her the food or the drink!

☐ F   Simple conversations, manners and politeness, kindness and thoughtfulness have all been replaced with a short, cold message on a screen.

☐ G   Nobody sends birthday cards anymore, except my grandma and even she is starting to use social media.

☐ H   Instead of talking and laughing together, we just press buttons.

☐ I   Which would you rather do: type LOL on a screen or actually laugh out loud with your friends or family, together, in the same room?

2 Look at the sentences you have **not** ticked. Explain why you would **not** include each one in your answer.

....

....

3 Look again at the sentences you have ticked. Which order (A, B, C etc.) would you put them in to build an effective response to the question?

....

Improve the answer

1 Write an improved answer to the question below. Use the hints to make sure your answer achieves the highest possible mark. Continue on a second sheet of paper if needed.

05 'Computers and phones rule everything we do. We can't think without them, go anywhere without them, or live without them. Technology has taken over our lives.'

Write an article for a broadsheet newspaper in which you explain your point of view on this statement.

(24 marks for content and organisation
16 marks for technical accuracy)

[40 marks]

Had a go

Everyone has got a phone and a computer. Everyone uses them all the time. If they weren't useful, nobody would buy them or use them. Some people say we should turn our phones off every now and then, but I disagree.

> **Hints**
>
> To present your point of view, each paragraph in the main body of your writing needs to do the following:
> * make a developed key point that will help to explain your point of view
> * use evidence to support the key point – this could be a fact, or an example from your own experience
> * clearly explain how this point and evidence support your point of view, helping the reader to understand and agree with your point of view.
>
> There are three opportunities for improvement in the first paragraph: the key point, the evidence and the explanation could all be more fully developed.

....

....

....

....

....

....

....

....

....

....

....

....

....

Connect the comments

1 Three students have written answers to the following question. Draw lines to connect each of the marker's comments to the relevant conclusion.

05 'Computers and phones rule everything we do. We can't think without them, go anywhere without them, or live without them. Technology has taken over our lives.'

Write an article for a broadsheet newspaper in which you explain your point of view on this statement.

(24 marks for content and organisation
16 marks for technical accuracy)
[40 marks]

Don't just repeat your main ideas in your conclusion. You need to summarise your point of view and explain the benefits of agreeing with it. You could also explain the problems people will face if they ignore your point of view!

Conclusion A

Technology helps us to communicate, it helps us to look after ourselves and it helps us to look after each other. We can use it to find out about the world and to change the world. It informs us, it entertains us, and it brings us closer together. If technology has all these benefits, why should we worry that it is playing such a big part in our lives? Technology is our slave, not our master.

There is a limited sense of reaching a conclusion in this final paragraph. Although it makes the writer's point of view clear, it simply repeats key points already made in the main body of the article and does not develop them. A limited range of vocabulary and sentence forms reduces its impact.

Conclusion B

As I have already said, technology can be a good thing but it can also be a bad thing. It can help us in our lives but if we use it too much we will have to rely on it for everything we do and, as I said earlier, what happens if it goes wrong? Overall, I think technology is a good thing but we should not rely on it too much.

The writer introduces a new idea in this conclusion, summarising earlier ideas about technology to consider its role in the future. A limited range of vocabulary reduces the impact of the writer's point of view, although there is some use of sentence forms for effect.

Conclusion C

Technology may have many advantages and there are lots of things it can do. However, we should always think about the negative effects it can have on our lives. As technology develops in the future, there may be many more negative effects and problems we cannot imagine, for example computers developing minds of their own and taking over. I think we should be careful.

This conclusion effectively summarises the writer's key ideas, making effective use of a variety of vocabulary and sentence forms for effect. The final sentences engage the reader, encouraging a response in agreement with the writer's view.

Improve the answer

1 Improve the paragraph below. Use the hints to make sure your paragraph achieves the highest possible mark. Continue on a second sheet of paper if needed.

05 'Computers and phones rule everything we do. We can't think without them, go anywhere without them, or live without them. Technology has taken over our lives.'

Write an article for a broadsheet newspaper in which you explain your point of view on this statement.

(24 marks for content and organisation
16 marks for technical accuracy)
[40 marks]

Nearly there

Everything would be different without technology. Imagine it. First, you wake up late because you haven't got an alarm. You don't even have a phone to tell your boss or friend you're going to be late for work or school. How are you supposed to get there quickly when there are no cars? You need to find another way to get to work but you can't look it up because there is no internet! So you walk to school, sit in lessons while the teacher talks at you because there are no computers or videos. Then you walk home and look at the walls because there is nothing else to do. Everything is better with technology.

Hints

To present your point of view effectively and engage your reader, think about the vocabulary you choose and how you can use language devices to give additional impact to your ideas. For example, you could use the following features:

- emotive language
- alliteration
- rhetorical questions
- lists or triple structures.

....
....
....
....
....
....
....
....
....
....
....

Mark the answer

1 Draw lines to connect each of the marker's comments to a relevant part (or parts) of this student's answer. One has been done for you.

05 'Computers and phones rule everything we do. We can't think without them, go anywhere without them, or live without them. Technology has taken over our lives.'

Write an article for a broadsheet newspaper in which you explain your point of view on this statement.

(24 marks for content and organisation
16 marks for technical accuracy)

[40 marks]

A recent survey showed that teenagers would rather give up choclate than give up their phones for a week and it also showed that the avarage teenager spends up to six hours a day on their phones, this shows how much their lives are ruled by technology. If there was more for teenagers to do then they proberly would not spend so much time staring at their phones. They might go out and enjoy themselves and get some fresh air.

A limited range of sentence forms are used.

Full stops and other sentence demarcation are not consistently accurate. (You only need to provide one example of this.)

Vocabulary choices are somewhat varied. (× 2)

Spelling of some common words is inaccurate. (× 3)

2 Draw lines to connect each of the marker's comments to a relevant part (or parts) of this student's answer. One has been done for you.

Technology is designed to take over our lives. If you have ever played a console or computer game, you will know how hours can last seconds and whole days can dissappear as you battle against aliens or enemy soldiers or cartoon characters in cars. Games are made for addiction. However, how many hours did we spend playing games before technology took over? A simple game of Monopoly can last an entire afternoon. My dad can spend half an hour staring at a chess board, trying to decide which little wooden figure to move a whole square forward – and that's just one move in a game that can last a whole day. Technology hasn't taken over our lives. It's just changed the things we do and the way we do them.

A range of sentence forms are crafted for effect.

Full stops and other sentence demarcation are accurate. (You only need to provide one example of this.)

A broad range of vocabulary choices. (× 2)

Spelling of some words is inaccurate.

Where an example answer is given, this is not necessarily the only correct response. In most cases, there is a range of responses that can gain full marks.

In questions that have more than one correct answer, you will see the (Suggested answer) stamp.

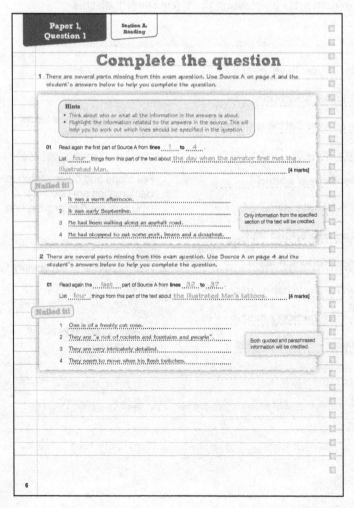

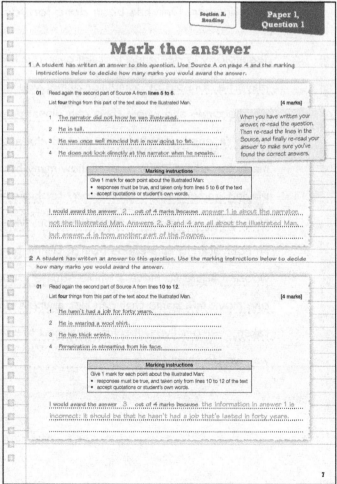

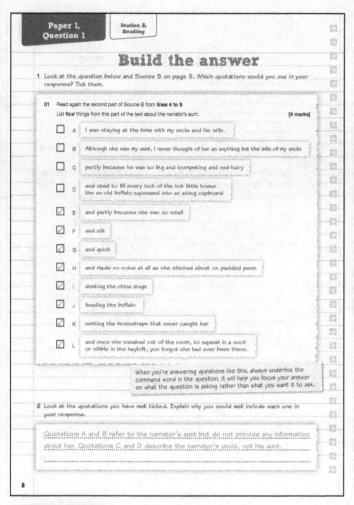

Paper 1, Question 1 — Section A: Reading

Build the answer

1 Look at the question below and Source B on page 5. Which quotations would you use in your response? Tick them.

01 Read again the second part of Source B from **lines 4 to 9**.
List **four** things from this part of the text about the narrator's aunt. **[4 marks]**

- ☐ A I was staying at the time with my uncle and his wife.
- ☐ B Although she was my aunt, I never thought of her as anything but the wife of my uncle
- ☐ C partly because he was so big and trumpeting and red-hairy
- ☐ D and used to fill every inch of the hot little house like an old buffalo squeezed into an airing cupboard
- ☑ E and partly because she was so small
- ☑ F and silk
- ☑ G and quick
- ☑ H and made no noise at all as she whisked about on padded paws
- ☑ I dusting the china dogs
- ☑ J feeding the buffalo
- ☑ K setting the mousetraps that never caught her
- ☑ L and once she sneaked out of the room, to squeak in a nook or nibble in the hayloft, you forgot she had ever been there.

> When you're answering questions like this, always underline the command word in the question. It will help you focus your answer on what the question is asking rather than what you want it to ask.

2 Look at the quotations you have **not** ticked. Explain why you would **not** include each one in your response.

Quotations A and B refer to the narrator's aunt but do not provide any information about her. Quotations C and D describe the narrator's uncle, not his aunt.

8

Section A: Reading — **Paper 1, Question 2**

Complete the question

1 There are several parts missing from this exam question. Use Source A on page 4 and the extracts from the three student responses below to complete the question.

02 Look in detail at lines 5 to 12 of Source A.
How does the writer use language here to present the Illustrated Man? *Suggested answer*

You could include the writer's choice of:
- words and phrases
- language features and techniques
- sentence forms.

> I always highlight the part of the Source I'm being asked to write about before answering the question.

[8 marks]

Nailed it!

Student A The writer presents the Illustrated Man as a mysterious character, describing his "wool shirt" being buttoned "tight" around his neck with his sleeves "rolled and buttoned down" even though it is a hot day. These descriptive adjectives and phrases create intrigue and make the reader speculate about why the Illustrated Man is dressed in this way and what he might be hiding.

Student B The Illustrated Man is shown as a huge person who might have once looked impressive. The writer uses a range of adjectives to describe him as "tall" and "once well muscled" with "long" arms and "thick" hands. These adjectives give the impression of a vast, strong man, which could suggest that he is a threatening or dangerous character to meet in an isolated place like this.

Student C The writer compares his face to "a child's" suggesting he is young at heart or perhaps innocent like a child and not worried about the troubles and problem he has faced in his life. This contrast with his huge body makes him a strange and interesting character for the reader.

2 Use the extracts from the three student responses below to complete this question.

02 Look in detail at lines 21 to 25 of Source A.
How does the writer use language here to show the Illustrated Man's thoughts and feelings? *Suggested answer*

You could include the writer's choice of:
- words and phrases
- language features and techniques
- sentence forms.

[8 marks]

Nailed it!

Student A The writer describes how he undoes his shirt "slowly" then with a "slow hand". This repetition emphasises how reluctant he feels about showing his tattoo.

Student B The Illustrated Man explains that he walks for hours in the sun hoping that "my sweat'll wash them off, the sun'll cook them off". Repeating this structure emphasises how desperate he feels about wanting to get rid of his tattoos.

Student C The Illustrated Man ends this explanation by asking "Are they still there now?" This short, simple question using simple, monosyllabic vocabulary adds emphasis to his desperation.

9

Paper 1, Question 2 — Section A: Reading

Connect the comments

1 Three students have written answers to Question 2 below. Draw lines to connect the marker's comments to the relevant answers.

02 Look in detail at **lines 5 to 12** of Source A.
How does the writer use language here to present the Illustrated Man?

You could include the writer's choice of:
- words and phrases
- language features and techniques
- sentence forms.

[8 marks]

Student A The writer uses a simile to describe the Illustrated Man's face, saying that it was "like a child's, set upon a massive body". Putting this contrast at the end of the sentence emphasises how mismatched these two things are, suggesting great strength but also the innocence and honesty of a child.

Student B The writer presents the Illustrated Man as a huge man who has got old and put on quite a lot of weight. It says he has a "massive body" and he was "once well muscled" but is now "going to fat". I don't think that the person telling the story knows why this happened though. I can tell this because he says "for some reason", which shows he doesn't know why.

Student C Throughout this part of the Source you get the impression that the Illustrated Man is hiding something. The writer says he "didn't look directly at me". The adverb "directly" makes me think he is avoiding eye contact because he is hiding something. In the same way, the Illustrated Man has perspiration "streaming from his face" because his shirt is "buttoned tight about his neck" and "buttoned down over his thick wrists". This also makes me think he is hiding something because it emphasises that he does not want to undo his shirt.

- The response shows some awareness of the writer's use of language and makes some reference to its effect, supported with relevant evidence. However the effect identified is not directly relevant to the focus of the question.

- The response shows some appreciation of a range of the writer's language choices, selecting relevant focused evidence and accurately using subject terminology to comment on its effect. Comments could be developed to analyse the writer's use of language in more detail.

- The response shows a clear and developed appreciation of the combined impact of the writer's choice of vocabulary and sentence form. This is focused on carefully chosen evidence and its effect is analysed in some detail with accurate use of subject terminology.

> Our English teacher told us that the best answers have detailed comments on the **effect** of the writer's choices of words, phrases, language techniques and sentence forms.

10

Section A: Reading — **Paper 1, Question 2**

Mark the answer

1 Draw lines to connect each of the marker's comments to a relevant part (or parts) of this student's answer. Two have been done for you.

02 Look in detail at **lines 21 to 25** of Source A.
How does the writer use language here to show the Illustrated Man's thoughts and feelings?

You could include the writer's choice of:
- words and phrases
- language features and techniques
- sentence forms.

[8 marks]

Suggested answer

The writer suggests that the Illustrated Man cannot even bear to look at his tattoos. As he undoes his shirt, he has "his eyes shut". The writer then repeats: "still shut". The adverb "still" emphasises the suggestion that he feels disgust and fear of the tattoos. The Illustrated Man also describes how he walks in the sun for hours "baking" hoping that "the sun'll cook them off". The verbs "bake" and "cook" highlight the pain he suffers just hoping to get rid of the tattoos. He ends by asking "Are they still there now?" In this short, single clause question the Illustrated Man shows his desperate hope that they will be gone.

- Makes some clear comments on the writer's vocabulary choices. (x 2)
- Ideas supported with relevant, focused textual evidence. (x 3)
- Comments on sentence form are clear and valid.
- Uses subject terminology accurately. (x 3)

2 Now use the mark scheme below to decide how many marks you would award the student's answer.

Level	Skills descriptors
Level 4 7–8 marks	Response demonstrates a developed and insightful appreciation of the writer's use of language: • clear and detailed analysis of the effect of the writer's language choices • a carefully selected range of relevant, focused textual evidence • a range of subject terminology to achieve clarity and precision.
Level 3 5–6 marks	Response demonstrates clear appreciation of the writer's use of language: • clear comments on the effect of the writer's language choices • a range of relevant, focused textual evidence • a range of subject terminology to achieve clarity.
Level 2 3–4 marks	Response demonstrates some appreciation of the writer's use of language: • some comments on the effect of the writer's language choices • relevant and focused textual evidence • largely accurate use of subject terminology.
Level 1 1–2 marks	Response demonstrates some awareness of the writer's use of language: • straightforward comments on the effect of the writer's language choices • largely relevant textual evidence • some use of subject terminology, with inconsistent accuracy.
Level 0 0 marks	No comments made on the writer's use of language. No rewardable response.

I would award the answer 7 out of 8 marks because the student makes *Suggested answer*
some clear, detailed comments on language, supported with a range of evidence and terminology, although the analysis could be more fully developed.

11

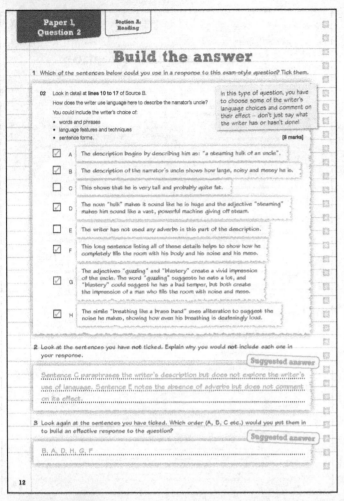

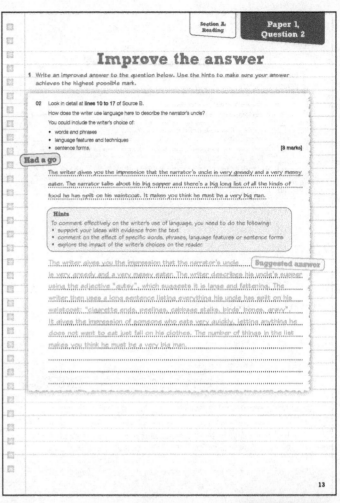

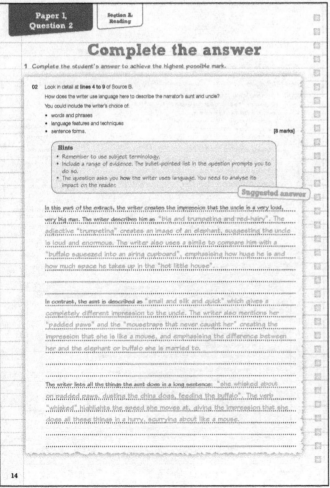

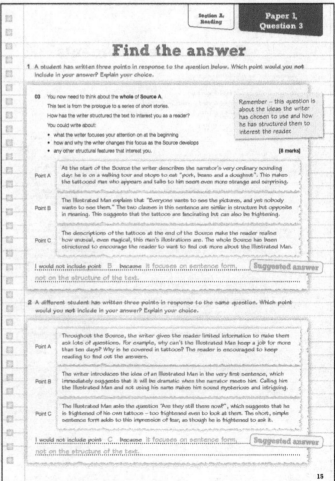

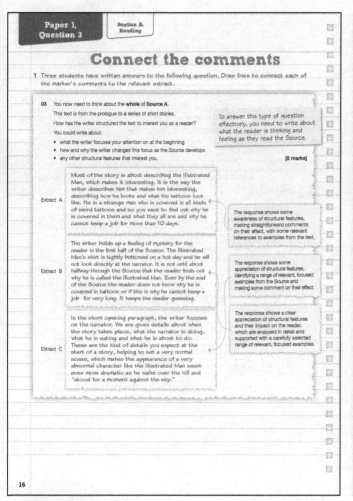

Connect the comments

1 Three students have written answers to the following question. Draw lines to connect each of the marker's comments to the relevant extract.

03 You now need to think about the **whole** of **Source A**.

This text is from the prologue to a series of short stories.

How has the writer structured the text to interest you as a reader?

You could write about:
- what the writer focuses your attention on at the beginning
- how and why the writer changes this focus as the Source develops
- any other structural features that interest you.

[8 marks]

> To answer this type of question effectively, you need to write about what the reader is thinking and feeling as they read the Source.

Extract A
Most of the story is about describing the Illustrated Man, which makes it interesting. It is in the way the writer describes him that makes him interesting, describing how he looks and what his tattoos look like. He is a strange man who is covered in all kinds of weird tattoos and so you want to find out why he is covered in them and what they all are and why he cannot keep a job for more than 10 days.

> The response shows some awareness of structural features, making straightforward comments on their effect, with some relevant references to examples from the text.

Extract B
The writer builds up a feeling of mystery for the reader in the first half of the Source. The Illustrated Man's shirt is tightly buttoned up and he will not look directly at the narrator. It is not until about halfway through the Source that the reader finds out why he is called the Illustrated Man. Even by the end of the Source the reader does not know why he is covered in tattoos or if this is why he cannot keep a job for very long. It keeps the reader guessing.

> The response shows some appreciation of structural features, identifying a range of relevant, focused examples from the Source and making some comment on their effect.

Extract C
In the short opening paragraph, the writer focuses on the narrator. We are given details about when the story takes place, what the narrator is doing, what he is eating and what he is about to do. These are the kind of details you expect at the start of a story, helping to set a very normal scene, which makes the appearance of a very abnormal character like the Illustrated Man seem even more dramatic as he walks over the hill and "stood for a moment against the sky."

> The response shows a clear appreciation of structural features and their impact on the reader, which are analysed in detail and supported with a carefully selected range of relevant, focused examples.

16

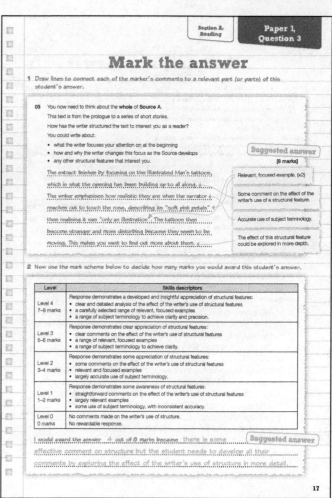

Mark the answer

1 Draw lines to connect each of the marker's comments to a relevant part (or parts) of this student's answer.

03 You now need to think about the **whole** of **Source A**.

This text is from the prologue to a series of short stories.

How has the writer structured the text to interest you as a reader?

You could write about:
- what the writer focuses your attention on at the beginning
- how and why the writer changes this focus as the Source develops
- any other structural features that interest you.

[8 marks]

> **Suggested answer**

The extract finishes by focusing on the Illustrated Man's tattoo, which is what the opening has been building up to all along. The writer emphasises how realistic they are when the narrator reaches out to touch the rose, describing its "soft pink petals" then realising it was "only an illustration". The tattoos then become stranger and more disturbing because they seem to be moving. This makes you want to find out more about them.

> Relevant, focused example. (x2)
> Some comment on the effect of the writer's use of a structural feature.
> Accurate use of subject terminology.
> The effect of this structural feature could be explored in more depth.

2 Now use the mark scheme below to decide how many marks you would award this student's answer.

Level	Skills descriptors
Level 4 7–8 marks	Response demonstrates a developed and insightful appreciation of structural features: • clear and detailed analysis of the effect of the writer's use of structural features • a carefully selected range of relevant, focused examples • a range of subject terminology to achieve clarity and precision.
Level 3 5–6 marks	Response demonstrates clear appreciation of structural features and their impact on the reader: • clear comments on the effect of the writer's use of structural features • a range of relevant, focused examples • a range of subject terminology to achieve clarity.
Level 2 3–4 marks	Response demonstrates some appreciation of structural features: • some comments on the effect of the writer's use of structural features • relevant and focused examples • largely accurate use of subject terminology.
Level 1 1–2 marks	Response demonstrates some awareness of structural features: • straightforward comments on the effect of the writer's use of structural features • largely relevant examples • some use of subject terminology, with inconsistent accuracy.
Level 0 0 marks	No comments made on the writer's use of structure. No rewardable response.

> **Suggested answer**

I would award the answer 4 out of 8 marks because there is some effective comment on structure but the student needs to develop all their comments by exploring the effect of the writer's use of structure in more detail.

17

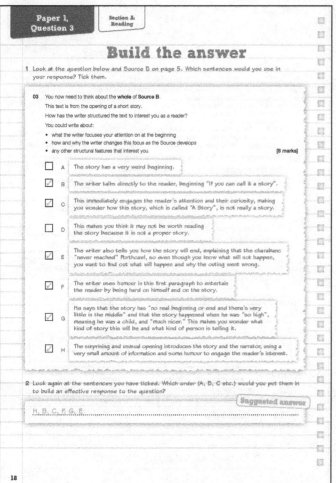

Build the answer

1 Look at the question below and Source B on page 5. Which sentences would you use in your response? Tick them.

03 You now need to think about the **whole** of **Source B**.

This text is from the opening of a short story.

How has the writer structured the text to interest you as a reader?

You could write about:
- what the writer focuses your attention on at the beginning
- how and why the writer changes this focus as the Source develops
- any other structural features that interest you.

[8 marks]

☐ A The story has a very weird beginning.

☑ B The writer talks directly to the reader, beginning "If you can call it a story".

☑ C This immediately engages the reader's attention and their curiosity, making you wonder how this story, which is called "A Story", is not really a story.

☐ D This makes you think it may not be worth reading the story because it is not a proper story.

☑ E The writer also tells you how the story will end, explaining that the charabanc "never reached" Porthcawl, so even though you know what will not happen, you want to find out what will happen and why the outing went wrong.

☑ F The writer uses humour in this first paragraph to entertain the reader by being hard on himself and on the story.

☑ G He says that the story has "no real beginning or end and there's very little in the middle" and that the story happened when he was "so high", meaning he was a child, and "much nicer." This makes you wonder what kind of story this will be and what kind of person is telling it.

☑ H The surprising and unusual opening introduces the story and the narrator, using a very small amount of information and some humour to engage the reader's interest.

2 Look again at the sentences you have ticked. Which order (A, B, C etc.) would you put them in to build an effective response to the question?

> **Suggested answer**

H, B, C, F, G, E

18

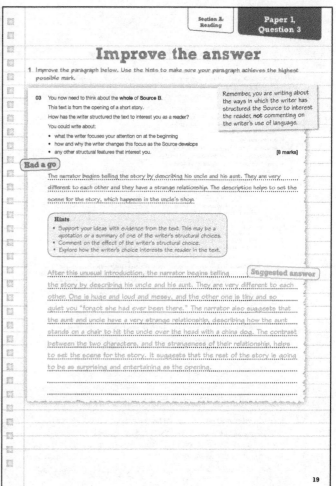

Improve the answer

1 Improve the paragraph below. Use the hints to make sure your paragraph achieves the highest possible mark.

03 You now need to think about the **whole** of **Source B**.

This text is from the opening of a short story.

How has the writer structured the text to interest you as a reader?

You could write about:
- what the writer focuses your attention on at the beginning
- how and why the writer changes this focus as the Source develops
- any other structural features that interest you.

[8 marks]

> Remember, you are writing about the ways in which the writer has structured the Source to interest the reader, **not** commenting on the writer's use of language.

> **Had a go**

The narrator begins telling the story by describing his uncle and his aunt. They are very different to each other and they have a strange relationship. The description helps to set the scene for the story, which happens in the uncle's shop.

Hints
- Support your ideas with evidence from the text. This may be a quotation or a summary of one of the writer's structural choices.
- Comment on the effect of the writer's structural choice.
- Explore how the writer's choice interests the reader in the text.

> **Suggested answer**

After this unusual introduction, the narrator begins telling the story by describing his uncle and his aunt. They are very different to each other. One is huge and loud and messy, and the other one is tiny and so quiet you "forgot she had ever been there." The narrator also suggests that the aunt and uncle have a very strange relationship, describing how the aunt stands on a chair to hit the uncle over the head with a china dog. The contrast between the two characters, and the strangeness of their relationship, helps to set the scene for the story. It suggests that the rest of the story is going to be as surprising and entertaining as the opening.

19

Paper 1, Question 3 — Section A: Reading

Complete the answer

1 Complete the student's answer to achieve the highest possible mark.

> 03 You now need to think about the **whole** of **Source B**.
> This text is from the opening of a short story.
> How has the writer structured the text to interest you as a reader?
> You could write about:
> * what the writer focuses your attention on at the beginning
> * how and why the writer changes this focus as the Source develops
> * any other structural features that interest you. **[8 marks]**
>
> **Hints**
> * Your answer should focus on the text at a structural level, not at a language level.
> * Use the bullet-pointed list in the question to help you structure your answer.
> * Remember to use subject terminology.

Suggested answer

In the first paragraph of the story, the writer grabs the reader's interest with a surprising opening that suggests this will be a very unusual story with "no real beginning or end". He also reveals that the story is about a visit to Porthcawl but hints that the characters will never reach their destination. The opening has been structured to intrigue the reader, making you want to find out what kind of story this will be and what problems will happen on their journey.

The writer then goes on to describe the narrator's aunt and uncle, creating humour by contrasting the huge, loud uncle with the tiny, silent aunt. The description of these two very different characters and their relationship is so strange that it draws you into the story, making you want to see what other strange characters and events will follow.

The story then moves on to describe the Illustrated Man uncle's friends come to to visit. The writer introduces conflict between the friends as they plan their outing because they obviously do not trust Mr Benjamin Franklyn who is supposed to be looking after the money to pay for the outing. This argument reminds the reader that they will never reach Porthcawl and so you begin to wonder if this could be the reason why, or if there will be even bigger problems later in the story. The whole of this opening has been structured to make you want to find out more.

Section A: Reading — Paper 1, Question 4

Complete the question

1 There are several parts missing from this exam question. Use Source A on page 4 and the extracts from the three student responses below to complete the question.

> 04 Focus this part of your answer on the _____second_____ part of Source A from line __18__ to __the end__.
> A student, having read this section of the text said: "_The writer's description of_ **Suggested answer** _the tattoos makes them fascinating but also disturbing. It is as if they are alive._"
> To what extent do you agree?
> In your response, you could:
> * write about your own impressions of _the Illustrated Man's tattoos_
> * evaluate how the writer has created these impressions
> * support your opinions with references to the text. **[20 marks]**

Nailed it!

Student A | The first way in which the writer makes the tattoos seem fascinating is the description of the rose, which is so realistic that the narrator thinks he can touch it. The writer effectively describes it as though it were a real rose, writing that it has been "freshly cut" with "drops of crystal water" on its "soft pink petals". The writer not only goes into detail about what the rose looks like but also how it feels, which shows the reader how realistic it looks. This description makes you think that they must be very good tattoos, or perhaps that there is something strange or magical about them.

Student B | Although the writer's description of the tattoos themselves is interesting, it is the way in which the effect that they have had on the Illustrated Man's life is explained that makes them really fascinating and equally disturbing. Even before the reader finds out what they look like, the writer makes it clear that they have ruined this man's life. The reader finds out that children follow the Illustrated Man around and that he can only "keep a job about ten days". All of these details are effective in making you realise that there is something disturbing about the tattoos.

Student C | The writer's clear and detailed description of the way the people in the tattoos seem to be moving makes them fascinating and disturbing. The writer lists all the different movements the narrator sees in a series of clauses to suggest them all moving at the same time: the flesh "twitched", the mouths "flickered", the eyes "winked" and the hands "gestured". These action verbs vividly create the impression of small movements adding up to the impression of a constantly changing picture. The writer also describes the "crowds that inhabited his body". The verb "inhabited" is a kind of personification that brings the images to life, suggesting that they are living people who live on the Illustrated Man's skin, which is the most disturbing idea in the whole extract.

Paper 1, Question 4 — Section A: Reading

Find the answer

1 A student has written three paragraphs in response to the question below. Which paragraph would you include in your answer? Explain your choice. Then, explain why you would **not** include the other two paragraphs.

> 04 Focus this part of your answer on the second part of Source A from **line 18 to the end**.
> A student, having read this section of the text said: "The writer makes you feel sorry for the Illustrated Man. You can see why his tattoos have caused him so many problems."
> To what extent do you agree?
> In your response, you could:
> * write about your own impressions of the Illustrated Man and his tattoos
> * evaluate how the writer has created these impressions
> * support your opinions with references to the text. **[20 marks]**

> Evaluation questions like this usually ask you to focus on half the Source, so make sure you only include in your answer references from the relevant part of the text.

Paragraph A | The writer is successful in making you feel sorry for the Illustrated Man by explaining how desperately the Illustrated Man is trying to keep his tattoos covered up. The writer effectively shows how hot it is, describing the Man's perspiration "streaming from his face", and emphasises that he is wearing a thick, warm "wool" shirt, which is "buttoned tight" around his neck and "buttoned down" around his wrists. In this way the writer makes it obvious that the Illustrated Man wants to keep himself covered up because he has something to hide.

Paragraph B | The writer describes the tattoos as "a riot of rockets and fountains and people". The metaphor "a riot" makes it sound like there are hundreds of tattoos crowded together, fighting for space. The description contrasts "rockets", which suggest power and violence with "fountains", which suggest peace and beauty, showing how different all the tattoos are. It's as if the man is illustrated with a whole world of tattoos.

Paragraph C | The writer most successfully makes the reader feel sorry for the Illustrated Man when he writes about how the Illustrated Man has tried to remove his tattoos. He describes walking "for hours" and "baking" hoping that his "sweat'll wash them off, the sun'll cook them off", which shows the pain he is prepared to go through to try to get rid of them. However, the reader knows this will not work, which makes the Illustrated Man seem even more hopeless and trapped by his tattoos.

I would include paragraph C because it answers the question effectively. It successfully evaluates how the writer makes the reader feel sympathetic towards the Illustrated Man.

I would not include paragraphs A or B because paragraph A focuses on the wrong part of the Source and paragraph B does not evaluate how well the writer has made the reader feel sorry for the Illustrated Man or why the tattoos have caused him so many problems.

Section A: Reading — Paper 1, Question 4

Mark the answer

1 Draw lines to connect each of the marker's comments to a relevant part of this student's answer.

> 04 Focus this part of your answer on the second part of Source A from **line 18 to the end**.
> A student, having read this section of the text said: "The writer's description of the tattoos makes them fascinating but also disturbing. It is as if they are alive."
> To what extent do you agree?
> In your response, you could:
> * write about your own impressions of the Illustrated Man's tattoos
> * evaluate how the writer has created these impressions
> * support your opinions with references to the text. **[20 marks]**

Suggested answer

The description of the tattoos is fascinating from the moment the Illustrated Man reveals them. The narrator says he is "covered with illustrations" and describes the "blue tattooed ring about his neck". The word "ring" makes it sound like a solid line of tattoo all around his neck, which emphasises how completely he is covered. The man himself then goes on to say that "All of me is illustrated." So the first impression you get is of a man who is completely covered in tattoos from his head to his feet. The writer also describes them as "a riot", which means there are a lot of them.

Markers comments:
- Response is focused on the statement in the question.
- Ideas supported with a range of relevant, focused textual evidence.
- Makes some clear comments on the writer's choices.
- Some effective evaluation of the effect of the writer's choices on the reader.
- Limited evaluation of the effect of the writer's choices on the reader.

2 Now use the mark scheme below to decide how many marks you would award the answer.

Level	Skills descriptors	
Level 4 16–20 marks	Response demonstrates developed and insightful evaluation: • clear and detailed analysis of the writer's choices • clear and full evaluation of the effect on the reader	• a carefully selected range of relevant, focused textual evidence • a developed and considered critical response to the statement.
Level 3 11–15 marks	Response demonstrates clear and focused evaluation: • clear comments on the writer's choices • clear evaluation of the effect on the reader	• a range of relevant, focused textual evidence • a relevant, focused response to the statement.
Level 2 6–10 marks	Response demonstrates inconsistently focused evaluation: • some comments on the writer's choices • some evaluation of their effect on the reader	• relevant and focused textual evidence • a more developed response to the statement.
Level 1 1–5 marks	Response demonstrates limited, straightforward evaluation: • straightforward comments on the writer's choices • straightforward evaluation of their effect on the reader	• largely relevant textual evidence • a straightforward response to the statement.
Level 0 0 marks	No comments made on the writer's choices, no evaluation, and no response to the statement. No rewardable response.	

I would award the answer 5 out of 20 marks because the student makes **Suggested answer** some clear comments on language, supported with evidence. However, their comments lack detail and development, and do not fully address the statement in the question.

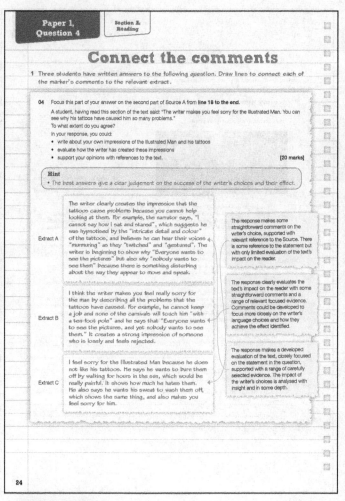

Connect the comments

1 Three students have written answers to the following question. Draw lines to connect each of the marker's comments to the relevant extract.

04 Focus this part of your answer on the second part of Source A from **line 18** to the end.

A student, having read this section of the text said: "The writer makes you feel sorry for the Illustrated Man. You can see why his tattoos have caused him so many problems."

To what extent do you agree?

In your response, you could:
- write about your own impressions of the Illustrated Man and his tattoos
- evaluate how the writer has created these impressions
- support your opinions with references to the text.

[20 marks]

Hint
- The best answers give a clear judgement on the success of the writer's choices and their effect.

Extract A
The writer clearly creates the impression that the tattoos cause problems because you cannot help looking at them. For example, the narrator says, "I cannot say how I sat and stared", which suggests he was hypnotised by the "intricate detail and colour" of the tattoos, and believes he can hear their voices "murmuring" as they "twitched" and "gestured". The writer is beginning to show why "Everyone wants to see the pictures" but also why "nobody wants to see them" because there is something disturbing about the way they appear to move and speak.

The response makes some straightforward comments on the writer's choice, supported with relevant reference to the Source. There is some reference to the statement but with only limited evaluation of the text's impact on the reader.

Extract B
I think the writer makes you feel really sorry for the man by describing all the problems that the tattoos have caused. For example, he cannot keep a job and none of the carnival will touch him "with a ten-foot pole" and he says that "Everyone wants to see the pictures, and yet nobody wants to see them." It creates a strong impression of someone who is lonely and feels rejected.

The response clearly evaluates the text's impact on the reader with some straightforward comments and a range of relevant focused evidence. Comments could be developed to focus more closely on the writer's language choices and how they achieve the effect identified.

Extract C
I feel sorry for the Illustrated Man because he does not like his tattoos. He says he wants to burn them off by walking for hours in the sun, which would be really painful. It shows how much he hates them. He also says he wants his sweat to wash them off, which shows the same thing, and also makes you feel sorry for him.

The response makes a developed evaluation of the text, closely focused on the statement in the question, supported with a range of carefully selected evidence. The impact of the writer's choices is analysed with insight and in some depth.

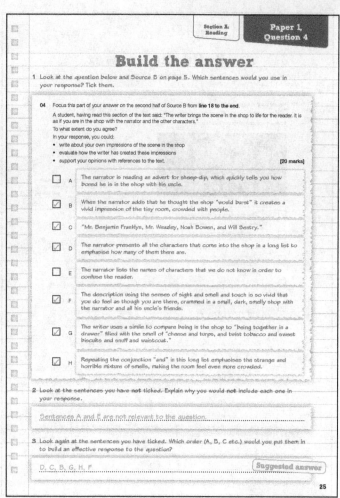

Build the answer

1 Look at the question below and Source B on page 5. Which sentences would you use in your response? Tick them.

04 Focus this part of your answer on the second half of Source B from **line 18** to the end.

A student, having read this section of the text said: "The writer brings the scene in the shop to life for the reader. It is as if you are in the shop with the narrator and the other characters."

To what extent do you agree?

In your response, you could:
- write about your own impressions of the scene in the shop
- evaluate how the writer has created these impressions
- support your opinions with references to the text.

[20 marks]

☐ A The narrator is reading an advert for sheep-dip, which quickly tells you how bored he is in the shop with his uncle.

☑ B When the narrator adds that he thought the room "would burst" it creates a vivid impression of the tiny room, crowded with people.

☑ C "Mr. Benjamin Franklyn, Mr. Weazley, Noah Bowen, and Will Sentry."

☑ D The narrator presents all the characters that come into the shop in a long list to emphasise how many of them there are.

☐ E The narrator lists the names of characters that we do not know in order to confuse the reader.

☑ F The description using the senses of sight and smell and touch is so vivid that you do feel as though you are there, crammed in a small, dark, smelly shop with the narrator and all his uncle's friends.

☑ G The writer uses a simile to compare being in the shop to "being together in a drawer" filled with the smell of "cheese and turps, and twist tobacco and sweet biscuits and snuff and waistcoat."

☑ H Repeating the conjunction "and" in this long list emphasises the strange and horrible mixture of smells, making the room feel even more crowded.

2 Look at the sentences you have **not** ticked. Explain why you would not include each one in your response.

Sentences A and E are not relevant to the question.

3 Look again at the sentences you have ticked. Which order (A, B, C etc.) would you put them in to build an effective response to the question?

Suggested answer

D, C, B, G, H, F

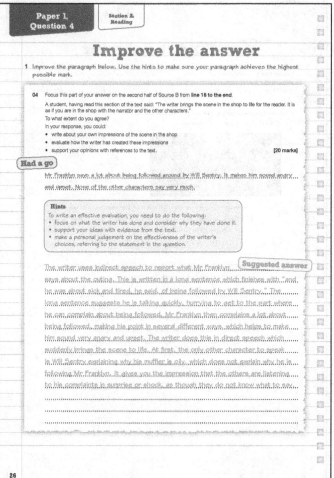

Improve the answer

1 Improve the paragraph below. Use the hints to make sure your paragraph achieves the highest possible mark.

04 Focus this part of your answer on the second half of Source B from **line 18** to the end.

A student, having read this section of the text said: "The writer brings the scene in the shop to life for the reader. It is as if you are in the shop with the narrator and the other characters."

To what extent do you agree?

In your response, you could:
- write about your own impressions of the scene in the shop
- evaluate how the writer has created these impressions
- support your opinions with references to the text.

[20 marks]

Had a go

Mr Franklyn says a lot about being followed around by Will Sentry. It makes him sound angry and upset. None of the other characters say very much.

Hints
To write an effective evaluation, you need to do the following:
- focus on what the writer has done and consider why they have done it.
- support your ideas with evidence from the text.
- make a personal judgement on the effectiveness of the writer's choices, referring to the statement in the question.

Suggested answer

The writer uses indirect speech to report what Mr Franklyn says about the outing. This is written in a long sentence which finishes with "and he was about sick and tired, he said, of being followed by Will Sentry." The long sentence suggests he is talking quickly, hurrying to get to the part where he can complain about being followed. Mr Franklyn then complains a lot about being followed, making his point in several different ways, which helps to make him sound very angry and upset. The writer does this in direct speech which suddenly brings the scene to life. At first, the only other character to speak is Will Sentry, explaining why his muffler is oily, which does not explain why he is following Mr Franklyn. It also gives you the impression that the others are listening to his complaints in surprise or shock, as though they do not know what to say.

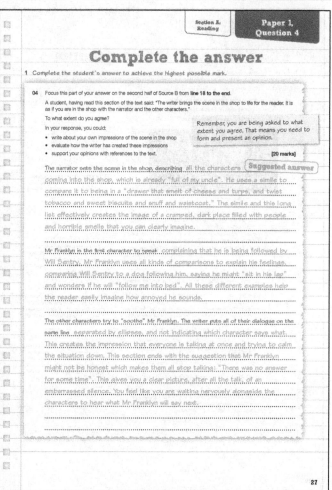

Complete the answer

1 Complete the student's answer to achieve the highest possible mark.

04 Focus this part of your answer on the second half of Source B from **line 18** to the end.

A student, having read this section of the text said: "The writer brings the scene in the shop to life for the reader. It is as if you are in the shop with the narrator and the other characters."

To what extent do you agree?

In your response, you could:
- write about your own impressions of the scene in the shop
- evaluate how the writer has created these impressions
- support your opinions with references to the text.

[20 marks]

Remember, you are being asked to what extent you agree. That means you need to form and present an opinion.

Suggested answer

The narrator sets the scene in the shop, describing all the characters coming into the shop, which is already "full of my uncle". He uses a simile to compare it to being in a "drawer that smelt of cheese and turps, and twist tobacco and sweet biscuits and snuff and waistcoat." The simile and this long list effectively creates the image of a cramped, dark place filled with people and horrible smells that you can clearly imagine.

Mr Franklyn is the first character to speak, complaining that he is being followed by Will Sentry. Mr Franklyn uses all kinds of comparisons to explain his feelings, comparing Will Sentry to a dog following him, saying he might "eat in his lap" and wonders if he will "follow me into bed". All these different examples help the reader easily imagine how annoyed he sounds.

The other characters try to "soothe" Mr Franklyn. The writer puts all of their dialogue on the same line, separated by ellipses, and not indicating which character says what. This creates the impression that everyone is talking at once and trying to calm the situation down. This section ends with the suggestion that Mr Franklyn might not be honest which makes them all stop talking: "There was no answer for some time". This gives you a clear picture, after all the talk, of an embarrassed silence. You feel like you are waiting nervously alongside the characters to hear what Mr Franklyn will say next.

Panel 1 (page 28)

Paper 1, Question 5 — **Section B: Writing**

Build the answer

1 Look at this question and the student's ideas below. Which ideas would you use in a plan to answer this question? Tick them.

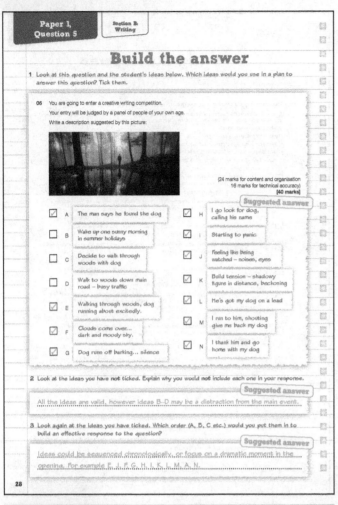

> 05 You are going to enter a creative writing competition.
> Your entry will be judged by a panel of people of your own age.
> Write a description suggested by this picture:
>
> (24 marks for content and organisation
> 16 marks for technical accuracy)
> [40 marks]

Suggested answer

☑	A	The man says he found the dog	☑	H	I go look for dog, calling his name
☐	B	Wake up one sunny morning in summer holidays	☑	I	Starting to panic
☐	C	Decide to walk through woods with dog	☑	J	Feeling like being watched – noises, eyes
☐	D	Walk to woods down main road – busy traffic	☑	K	Build tension – shadowy figure in distance, beckoning
☑	E	Walking through woods, dog running about excitedly.	☑	L	He's got my dog on a lead
☑	F	Clouds come over... dark and moody sky.	☑	M	I run to him, shouting give me back my dog
☑	G	Dog runs off barking... silence	☑	I	I thank him and go home with my dog

2 Look at the ideas you have not ticked. Explain why you would not include each one in your response.

Suggested answer

All the ideas are valid, however ideas B–D may be a distraction from the main event.

3 Look again at the ideas you have ticked. Which order (A, B, C etc.) would you put them in to build an effective response to the question?

Suggested answer

Ideas could be sequenced chronologically, or focus on a dramatic moment in the opening, for example F, J, F, G, H, I, K, L, M, N.

28

Panel 2 (page 29)

Section B: Writing — **Paper 1, Question 5**

Find the answer

1 Which of the openings below would you use to begin your answer to this question? Explain your choice. Then, explain why you would not use the other two openings.

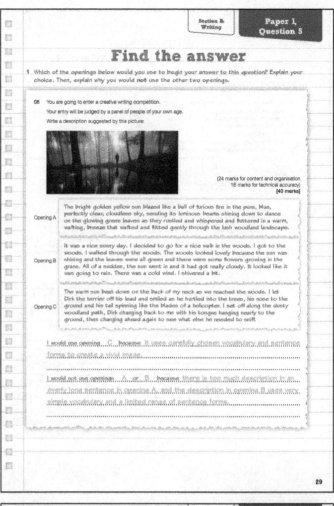

> 05 You are going to enter a creative writing competition.
> Your entry will be judged by a panel of people of your own age.
> Write a description suggested by this picture:
>
> (24 marks for content and organisation
> 16 marks for technical accuracy)
> [40 marks]

Opening A
The bright golden yellow sun blazed like a ball of furious fire in the pure, blue, perfectly clean, cloudless sky, sending its luminous beams shining down to dance on the glowing green leaves as they rustled and whispered and fluttered in a warm, wafting, breeze that wafted and flitted gently through the lush woodland landscape.

Opening B
It was a nice sunny day. I decided to go for a nice walk in the woods. I got to the woods. I walked through the woods. The woods looked lovely because the sun was shining and the leaves were all green and there were some flowers growing in the grass. All of a sudden, the sun went in and it had got really cloudy. It looked like it was going to rain. There was a cold wind. I shivered a bit.

Opening C
The warm sun beat down on the back of my neck as we reached the woods. I let Dirk the terrier off his lead and smiled as he hurtled into the trees, his nose to the ground and his tail spinning like the blades of a helicopter. I set off along the dusty woodland path, Dirk charging back to me with his tongue hanging nearly to the ground, then charging ahead again to see what else he needed to sniff.

I would use opening C because it uses carefully chosen vocabulary and sentence forms to create a vivid image.

I would not use openings A or B because there is too much description in an overly long sentence in opening A, and the description in opening B uses very simple vocabulary, and a limited range of sentence forms.

29

Panel 3 (page 30)

Paper 1, Question 5 — **Section B: Writing**

Connect the comments

1 Three students have written answers to the following question. Draw lines to connect each of the marker's comments to the relevant extract.

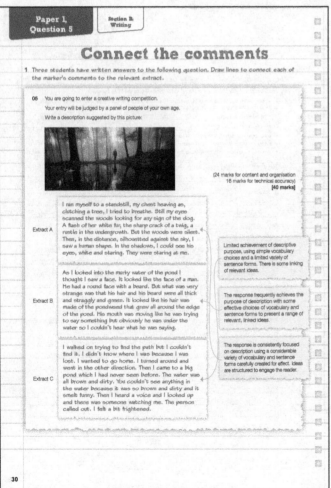

> 05 You are going to enter a creative writing competition.
> Your entry will be judged by a panel of people of your own age.
> Write a description suggested by this picture:
>
> (24 marks for content and organisation
> 16 marks for technical accuracy)
> [40 marks]

Extract A
I ran myself to a standstill, my chest heaving as, clutching a tree, I tried to breathe. Still my eyes scanned the woods looking for any sign of the dog. A flash of her white fur, the sharp crack of a twig, a rustle in the undergrowth. But the woods were silent. Then, in the distance, silhouetted against the sky, I saw a human shape. In the shadows, I could see his eyes, white and staring. They were staring at me.

> Limited achievement of descriptive purpose, using simple vocabulary choices and a limited variety of sentence forms. There is some linking of relevant ideas.

Extract B
As I looked into the murky water of the pond I thought I saw a face. It looked like the face of a man. He had a round face with a beard. But what was very strange was that his hair and his beard were all thick and straggly and green. It looked like his hair was made of the pondweed that grew all around the edge of the pond. His mouth was moving like he was trying to say something but obviously he was under the water so I couldn't hear what he was saying.

> The response frequently achieves the purpose of description with some effective choices of vocabulary and sentence forms to present a range of relevant, linked ideas.

Extract C
I walked on trying to find the path but I couldn't find it. I didn't know where I was because I was lost. I wanted to go home. I turned around and went in the other direction. Then I came to a big pond which I had never seen before. The water was all brown and dirty. You couldn't see anything in the water because it was so brown and dirty and it smelt funny. Then I heard a voice and I looked up and there was someone watching me. The person called out. I felt a bit frightened.

> The response is consistently focused on description using a considerable variety of vocabulary and sentence forms carefully created for effect. Ideas are structured to engage the reader.

30

Panel 4 (page 31)

Section B: Writing — **Paper 1, Question 5**

Find the answer

1 Look at the student responses to this question. Which response contains no spelling, punctuation or grammar errors? Tick it.
2 Then, cross out and correct any spelling, punctuation or grammar errors in the responses below.

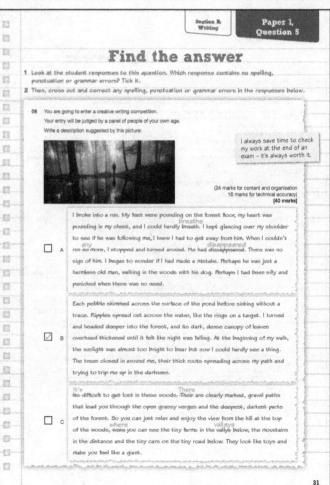

> 05 You are going to enter a creative writing competition.
> Your entry will be judged by a panel of people of your own age.
> Write a description suggested by this picture:
>
> (24 marks for content and organisation
> 16 marks for technical accuracy)
> [40 marks]

> I always save time to check my work at the end of an exam – it's always worth it.

☐ A
I broke into a run. My feet were pounding on the forest floor, my heart was pounding in my chest, and I could hardly breath. ~~breathe~~ I kept glancing over my shoulder to see if he was following me. I knew I had to get away from him. When I couldn't run no more, ~~any~~ I stopped and turned around. He had disappeared. ~~disappeared~~ There was no sign of him. I began to wonder if I had made a mistake. Perhaps he was just a harmless old man, walking in the woods with his dog. Perhaps I had been silly and panicked when there was no need.

☑ B
Each pebble skimmed across the surface of the pond before sinking without a trace. Ripples spread out across the water, like the rings on a target. I turned and headed deeper into the forest, and its dark, dense canopy of leaves overhead thickened until it felt like night was falling. At the beginning of my walk, the sunlight was almost too bright to bear but now I could hardly see a thing. The trees closed in around me, their thick roots spreading across my path and trying to trip me up in the darkness.

☐ C
Its difficult to get lost in these woods. ~~It's~~ Their clearly marked, gravel paths ~~There~~ that lead you through the open grassy verges and the deepest, darkest parts of the forest. So you can just relax and enjoy the view from the hill at the top of the woods, wars you can see the tiny farms in the vallys below, the mountains ~~where~~ ~~valleys~~ in the distance and the tiny cars on the tiny road below. They look like toys and make you feel like a giant.

31

82

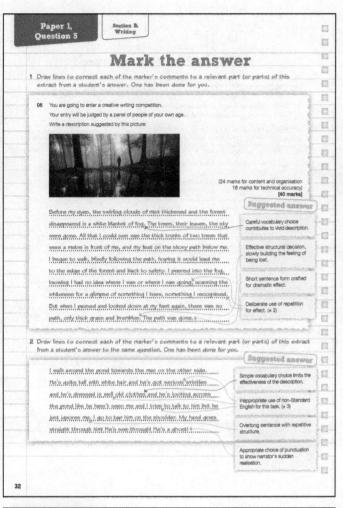

Mark the answer

1 Draw lines to connect each of the marker's comments to a relevant part (or parts) of this extract from a student's answer. One has been done for you.

05 You are going to enter a creative writing competition.
Your entry will be judged by a panel of people of your own age.
Write a description suggested by this picture:

(24 marks for content and organisation
16 marks for technical accuracy)
[40 marks]

Suggested answer

Before my eyes, the swirling clouds of mist thickened and the forest disappeared in a white blanket of fog. The trees, their leaves, the sky were gone. All that I could see was the thick trunks of two trees that were a metre in front of me, and my feet on the stony path below me. I began to walk, blindly following the path, hoping it would lead me to the edge of the forest and back to safety. I peered into the fog, knowing I had no idea where I was or where I was going, scanning the whiteness for a glimpse of something I knew, something I recognised. But when I paused and looked down at my feet again, there was no path, only thick grass and brambles. The path was done.

Careful vocabulary choice contributes to vivid description.

Effective structural decision, slowly building the feeling of being lost.

Short sentence form crafted for dramatic effect.

Deliberate use of repetition for effect. (x 2)

2 Draw lines to connect each of the marker's comments to a relevant part (or parts) of this extract from a student's answer to the same question. One has been done for you.

Suggested answer

I walk around the pond towards the man on the other side. He's quite tall with white hair and he's got serious wrinkles and he's dressed in well old clothes and he's looking across the pond like he hasn't seen me and I tries to talk to him but he just ignores me. I go to tap him on the shoulder. My hand goes straight through him! He's see-through! He's a ghost!!

Simple vocabulary choice limits the effectiveness of the description.

Inappropriate use of non-Standard English for this task. (x 3)

Overlong sentence with repetitive structure.

Appropriate choice of punctuation to show narrator's sudden realisation.

32

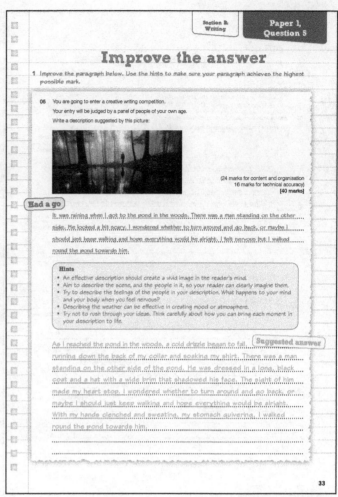

Improve the answer

1 Improve the paragraph below. Use the hints to make sure your paragraph achieves the highest possible mark.

05 You are going to enter a creative writing competition.
Your entry will be judged by a panel of people of your own age.
Write a description suggested by this picture:

(24 marks for content and organisation
16 marks for technical accuracy)
[40 marks]

Had a go

It was raining when I got to the pond in the woods. There was a man standing on the other side. He looked a bit scary. I wondered whether to turn around and go back, or maybe I should just keep walking and hope everything would be alright. I felt nervous but I walked round the pond towards him.

Hints
- An effective description should create a vivid image in the reader's mind.
- Aim to describe the scene, and the people in it, so your reader can clearly imagine them.
- Try to describe the feelings of the people in your description. What happens to your mind and your body when you feel nervous?
- Describing the weather can be effective in creating mood or atmosphere.
- Try not to rush through your ideas. Think carefully about how you can bring each moment in your description to life.

Suggested answer

As I reached the pond in the woods, a cold drizzle began to fall, running down the back of my collar and soaking my shirt. There was a man standing on the other side of the pond. He was dressed in a long, black coat and a hat with a wide brim that shadowed his face. The sight of him made my heart stop. I wondered whether to turn around and go back, or maybe I should just keep walking and hope everything would be alright. With my hands clenched and sweating, my stomach quivering, I walked round the pond towards him.

33

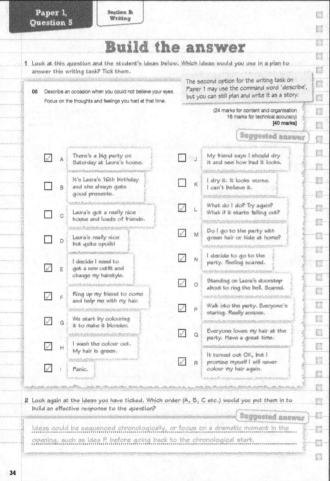

Build the answer

1 Look at this question and the student's ideas below. Which ideas would you use in a plan to answer this writing task? Tick them.

05 Describe an occasion when you could not believe your eyes.
Focus on the thoughts and feelings you had at that time.

The second option for the writing task on Paper 1 may use the command word 'describe', but you can still plan and write it as a story.

(24 marks for content and organisation
16 marks for technical accuracy)
[40 marks]

Suggested answer

A There's a big party on Saturday at Laura's house.

B It's Laura's 16th birthday and she always gets good presents.

C Laura's got a really nice house and loads of friends.

D Laura's really nice but quite spoilt!

E ✓ I decide I need to get a new outfit and change my hairstyle.

F ✓ Ring up my friend to come and help me with my hair.

G ✓ We start by colouring it to make it blonder.

H ✓ I wash the colour out. My hair is green.

I ✓ Panic.

J My friend says I should dry it and see how bad it looks.

K I dry it. It looks worse. I can't believe it.

L ✓ What do I do? Try again? What if it starts falling out?

M ✓ Do I go to the party with green hair or hide at home?

N ✓ I decide to go to the party, feeling scared.

O ✓ Standing on Laura's doorstep about to ring the bell. Scared.

P ✓ Walk into the party. Everyone's staring. Really anxious.

Q ✓ Everyone loves my hair at the party. Have a great time.

R ✓ It turned out OK, but I promise myself I will never colour my hair again.

2 Look again at the ideas you have ticked. Which order (A, B, C etc.) would you put them in to build an effective response to the question?

Suggested answer

Ideas could be sequenced chronologically, or focus on a dramatic moment in the opening, such as idea P, before going back to the chronological start.

34

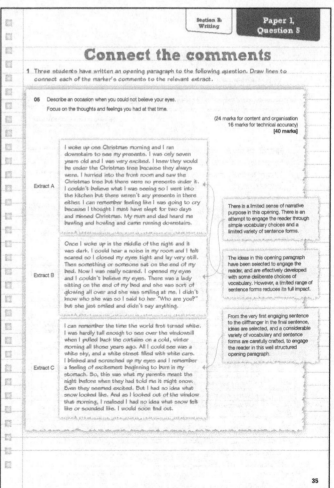

Connect the comments

1 Three students have written an opening paragraph to the following question. Draw lines to connect each of the marker's comments to the relevant extract.

05 Describe an occasion when you could not believe your eyes.
Focus on the thoughts and feelings you had at that time.

(24 marks for content and organisation
16 marks for technical accuracy)
[40 marks]

Extract A
I woke up one Christmas morning and I ran downstairs to see my presents. I was only seven years old and I was very excited. I knew they would be under the Christmas tree because they always were. I hurried into the front room and saw the Christmas tree but there were no presents under it. I couldn't believe what I was seeing so I went into the kitchen but there weren't any presents in there either. I can remember feeling like I was going to cry because I thought I must have slept for two days and missed Christmas. My mum and dad heard me bawling and howling and came running downstairs.

There is a limited sense of narrative purpose in this opening. There is an attempt to engage the reader through simple vocabulary choices and a limited variety of sentence forms.

Extract B
Once I woke up in the middle of the night and it was dark. I could hear a noise in my room and I felt scared so I closed my eyes tight and lay very still. Then something or someone sat on the end of my bed. Now I was really scared. I opened my eyes and I couldn't believe my eyes. There was a lady sitting on the end of my bed and she was sort of glowing all over and she was smiling at me. I didn't know who she was so I said to her "Who are you?" but she just smiled and didn't say anything.

The ideas in this opening paragraph have been selected to engage the reader, and are effectively developed with some deliberate choices of vocabulary. However, a limited range of sentence forms reduces its full impact.

Extract C
I can remember the time the world first turned white. I was hardly tall enough to see over the windowsill when I pulled back the curtains on a cold, winter morning all those years ago. All I could see was a white sky, and a white street filled with white cars. I blinked and scrunched up my eyes and I remember a feeling of excitement beginning to burn in my stomach. So, this was what my parents meant the night before when they had told me it might snow. Even they seemed excited. But I had no idea what snow looked like. And as I looked out of the window that morning, I realised I had no idea what snow felt like or sounded like. I would soon find out.

From the very first engaging sentence to the cliffhanger in the final sentence, ideas are selected, and a considerable variety of vocabulary and sentence forms are carefully crafted, to engage the reader in this well structured opening paragraph.

35

Paper 1, Question 5 — Section B: Writing

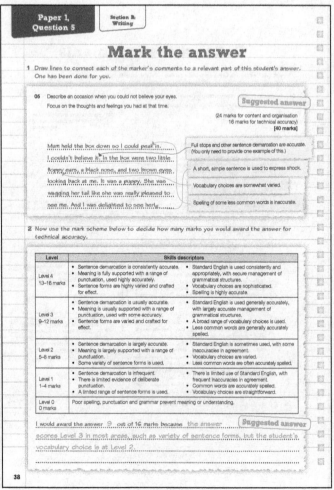

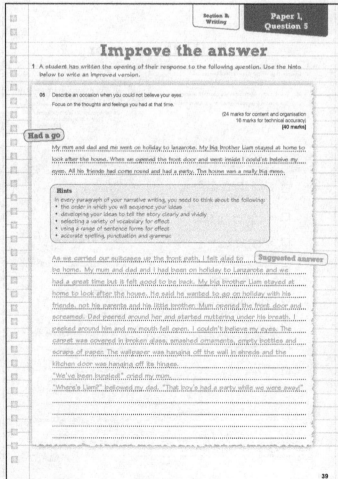

Paper 1, Question 5 — Section B: Writing

Complete the answer

1 Read this question then complete each student's plan by adding an effective ending for each of their stories.

> A good story needs to set the scene, involve a conflict or problem that builds up and reaches a crisis, and then provide a resolution or ending to finish it off.

05 Describe an occasion when you could not believe your eyes.
Focus on the thoughts and feelings you had at that time.

(24 marks for content and organisation
16 marks for technical accuracy)
[40 marks]

Student A
- I had been telling everyone for weeks it was nearly my 16th birthday.
- Woke up on my birthday. The house was empty. Note from my mum – "See you later".
- Hung around bored all day. My friend texted: meet me in the park. I went to meet her.
- When I got to the park, she texted me again: come *Suggested answer* back to your house. Surprise party when I got home.

Student B
- Woke up one Christmas morning when I was seven. Ran downstairs to open presents.
- No presents under the tree or anywhere else.
- Mum and Dad came in. It was like they had forgotten it was Christmas.
- Mum said she had suddenly remembered something. *Suggested answer* Went out of the room and came back with a cardboard box. There was a puppy in it!

Student C
- Very excited about going on holiday. Getting on the plane, getting to the hotel.
- The hotel is a dump. It looks like a building site. Our room smells. So disappointed.
- Go to bed that night. Dripping tap. Strange creaking noises.
- Leave the hotel the next morning, book into a much *Suggested answer* nicer one and have a great holiday.

36

Section B: Writing — Paper 1, Question 5

Re-order the answer

1 The sentences below are taken from a paragraph written by a student in response to the following question. Rearrange the sentences into the most logical order by numbering them from 1 to 5.

05 Describe an occasion when you could not believe your eyes.
Focus on the thoughts and feelings you had at that time.

(24 marks for content and organisation
16 marks for technical accuracy)
[40 marks]

> The first and last sentences of a paragraph are often the most important. The first one can grab the reader, and the last one can make them want to find out what happens next.

Suggested answer

- [1] As we reached the hotel and got out of the taxi, my heart sank.
- [5] But it was even worse than it looked.
- [3] Around the hotel, where there should have been grass and flowers, there was rubble and dust.
- [4] There were diggers and dumpers and bulldozers everywhere, none of them moving.
- [2] I remember wondering whether they hadn't finished building the hotel yet, or whether some of it had recently fallen down.

2 The sentences below are taken from a paragraph written by another student in response to the same question. Rearrange the sentences into the most logical order by numbering them from 1 to 5.

Suggested answer

- [4] I pushed the pillow up over my ears, closed my eyes as tightly as I could to try to go to sleep.
- [1] The thin curtains glowed with the lights from the street outside.
- [2] Music from the club next door thumped through the walls and made the floor shake.
- [5] Maybe, I thought, I'll wake up in the morning and find that this was all just a bad dream.
- [3] I could hear the water in the clanking pipes gurgling and the drip, drip, drip of the tap in the dirty bathroom.

37

Paper 1, Question 5 — Section B: Writing

Mark the answer

1 Draw lines to connect each of the marker's comments to a relevant part of this student's answer. One has been done for you.

05 Describe an occasion when you could not believe your eyes.
Focus on the thoughts and feelings you had at that time.

Suggested answer

(24 marks for content and organisation
16 marks for technical accuracy)
[40 marks]

Mum held the box down so I could peek in. I couldn't believe it. In the box were two little floppy ears, a black nose, and two brown eyes looking back at me. It was a puppy. She was wagging her tail like she was really pleased to see me. And I was delighted to see her.

- Full stops and other sentence demarcation are accurate. (You only need to provide one example of this.)
- A short, simple sentence is used to express shock.
- Vocabulary choices are somewhat varied.
- Spelling of some less common words is inaccurate.

2 Now use the mark scheme below to decide how many marks you would award the answer for technical accuracy.

Level	Skills descriptors	
Level 4 13–16 marks	• Sentence demarcation is consistently accurate. • Meaning is fully supported with a range of punctuation, used highly accurately. • Sentence forms are highly varied and crafted for effect.	• Standard English is used consistently and appropriately, with secure management of grammatical structures. • Vocabulary choices are sophisticated. • Spelling is highly accurate.
Level 3 9–12 marks	• Sentence demarcation is usually accurate. • Meaning is usually supported with a range of punctuation, used with some accuracy. • Sentence forms are varied and crafted for effect.	• Standard English is used generally accurately, with largely accurate management of grammatical structures. • A broad range of vocabulary choices is used. • Less common words are generally accurately spelled.
Level 2 5–8 marks	• Sentence demarcation is largely accurate. • Meaning is largely supported with a range of punctuation. • Some variety of sentence forms is used.	• Standard English is sometimes used, with some inaccuracies in agreement. • Vocabulary choices are varied. • Less common words are often accurately spelled.
Level 1 1–4 marks	• Sentence demarcation is infrequent. • There is limited evidence of deliberate punctuation. • A limited range of sentence forms is used.	• There is limited use of Standard English, with frequent inaccuracies in agreement. • Common words are accurately spelled. • Vocabulary choices are straightforward.
Level 0 0 marks	Poor spelling, punctuation and grammar prevent meaning or understanding.	

I would award the answer 9 out of 16 marks because the answer *Suggested answer* scores Level 3 in most areas, such as variety of sentence forms, but the student's vocabulary choice is at Level 2.

38

Section B: Writing — Paper 1, Question 5

Improve the answer

1 A student has written the opening of their response to the following question. Use the hints below to write an improved version.

05 Describe an occasion when you could not believe your eyes.
Focus on the thoughts and feelings you had at that time.

(24 marks for content and organisation
16 marks for technical accuracy)
[40 marks]

Had a go

My mum and dad and me went on holiday to lanzarote. My big brother Liam stayed at home to look after the house. When we opened the front door and went inside I could'nt believe my eyes. All his friends had come round and had a party. The house was a really big mess.

Hints
In every paragraph of your narrative writing, you need to think about the following:
- the order in which you will sequence your ideas
- developing your ideas to tell the story clearly and vividly
- selecting a variety of vocabulary for effect
- using a range of sentence forms for effect
- accurate spelling, punctuation and grammar.

As we carried our suitcases up the front path, I felt glad to *Suggested answer* be home. My mum and dad and I had been on holiday to Lanzarote and we had a great time but it felt good to be back. My big brother Liam stayed at home to look after the house. He said he wanted to go on holiday with his friends, not his parents and his little brother. Mum opened the front door and screamed. Dad peered around her and started muttering under his breath. I peeked around him and my mouth fell open. I couldn't believe my eyes. The carpet was covered in broken glass, smashed ornaments, empty bottles and scraps of paper. The wallpaper was hanging off the wall in shreds and the kitchen door was hanging off its hinges.
"We've been burgled!" cried my mum.
"Where's Liam?" bellowed my dad. "That boy's had a party while we were away!"

39

Paper 2, Question 1 — Section A: Reading

Complete the question

1 There are several parts missing from this exam question. Use Source C on page 40 and the answers the student has selected below to complete the question.

01 Read again the first part of **Source C**, from lines __1__ to __10__.

Choose __four__ statements below which are __true__.

You need to look for facts to answer this question. Just because someone's opinion is argued convincingly, it doesn't mean it is a fact.

- Shade the boxes of the ones that you think are __true__.
- Choose a maximum of __four__ statements. **[4 marks]**

Nailed it!

A Smartphones are used by older people as well as younger people.

B Smartphones have replaced lots of other devices.

C Smartphones are expensive to buy.

D Smartphone applications are used by a wide range of people and organisations to communicate and share information.

E Many schools have banned their students from using smartphones.

F Surveys show that we think we could not live without our smartphones.

G Older people find it difficult to use smartphones.

H Smartphones have made our lives much more difficult in some ways.

2 There are several parts missing from this exam question. Use Source C on page 40 and the answers the student has selected below to complete the question.

01 Read again the middle part of **Source C**, from lines __12__ to __24__.

Choose __four__ statements below which are __true__.

- Shade the boxes of the ones that you think are __true__.
- Choose a maximum of __four__ statements. **[4 marks]**

Nailed it!

A Some people worry that smartphones have changed the way we communicate.

B Everyone in a doctor's waiting room is looking at their smartphone.

C The smartphone has changed some people's lives.

D Smartphones have made our lives much more difficult in some ways.

E Smartphones have made us more selfish.

F The smartphone has made us more concerned about our appearance and what people think of us.

G The iPhone was invented in order to make money.

H Shy people prefer to travel long distances rather than use a smartphone.

44

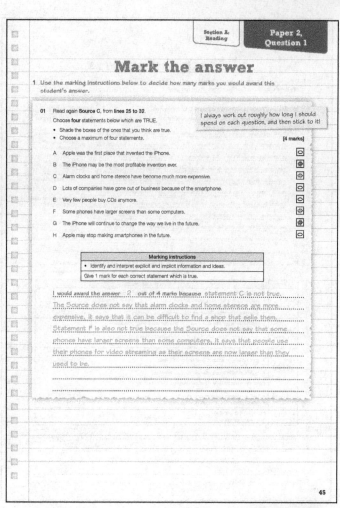

Section A: Reading — **Paper 2, Question 1**

Mark the answer

1 Use the marking instructions below to decide how many marks you would award this student's answer.

01 Read again **Source C**, from lines 25 to 32.

Choose **four** statements below which are TRUE.

I always work out roughly how long I should spend on each question, and then stick to it!

- Shade the boxes of the ones that you think are true.
- Choose a maximum of four statements. **[4 marks]**

A Apple was the first place that invented the iPhone.

B The iPhone may be the most profitable invention ever.

C Alarm clocks and home stereos have become much more expensive.

D Lots of companies have gone out of business because of the smartphone.

E Very few people buy CDs anymore.

F Some phones have larger screens than some computers.

G The iPhone will continue to change the way we live in the future.

H Apple may stop making smartphones in the future.

Marking instructions
• Identify and interpret explicit and implicit information and ideas.
Give 1 mark for each correct statement which is true.

I would award the answer __2__ out of 4 marks because statement C is not true. The Source does not say that alarm clocks and home stereos are more expensive, it says that it can be difficult to find a shop that sells them. Statement F is also not true because the Source does not say that some phones have larger screens than some computers, it says that people use their phones for video streaming as their screens are now larger than they used to be.

45

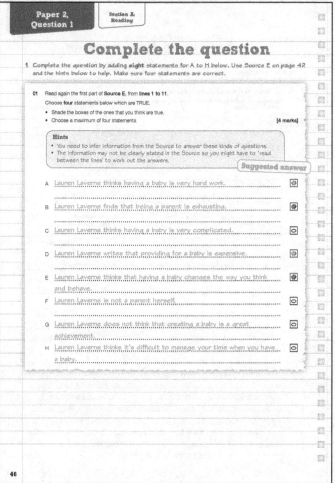

Paper 2, Question 1 — Section A: Reading

Complete the question

1 Complete the question by adding **eight** statements for A to H below. Use Source E on page 42 and the hints below to help. Make sure four statements are correct.

01 Read again the first part of **Source E**, from lines 1 to 11.

Choose **four** statements below which are TRUE.

- Shade the boxes of the ones that you think are true.
- Choose a maximum of four statements. **[4 marks]**

Hints
- You need to infer information from the Source to answer these kinds of questions.
- The information may not be clearly stated in the Source so you might have to 'read between the lines' to work out the answers.

Suggested answer

A Lauren Laverne thinks having a baby is very hard work.

B Lauren Laverne finds that being a parent is exhausting.

C Lauren Laverne thinks having a baby is very complicated.

D Lauren Laverne writes that providing for a baby is expensive.

E Lauren Laverne thinks that having a baby changes the way you think and behave.

F Lauren Laverne is not a parent herself.

G Lauren Laverne does not think that creating a baby is a great achievement.

H Lauren Laverne thinks it's difficult to manage your time when you have a baby.

46

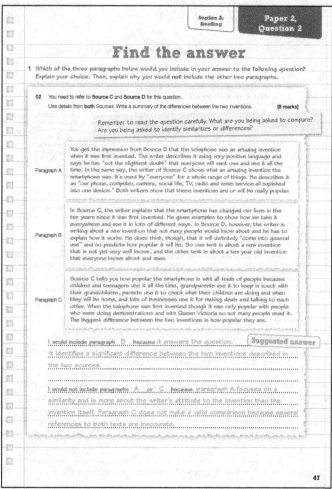

Section A: Reading — **Paper 2, Question 2**

Find the answer

1 Which of the three paragraphs below would you include in your answer to the following question? Explain your choice. Then, explain why you would **not** include the other two paragraphs.

02 You need to refer to **Source C** and **Source D** for this question.

Use details from **both** Sources. Write a summary of the differences between the two inventions. **[8 marks]**

Remember to read the question carefully. What are you being asked to compare? Are you being asked to identify similarities or differences?

Paragraph A You get the impression from Source D that the telephone was an amazing invention when it was first invented. The writer describes it using very positive language and says he has "not the slightest doubt" that everyone will want one and use it all the time. In the same way, the writer of Source C shows what an amazing invention the smartphone was. It's used by "everyone" for a whole range of things. He describes it as "our phone, computer, camera, social life, TV, radio and news service all squished into one device." Both writers show that these inventions are or will be really popular.

Paragraph B In Source C, the writer explains that the smartphone has changed our lives in the ten years since it was first invented. He gives examples to show how we take it everywhere and use it in lots of different ways. In Source D, however, the writer is writing about a new invention that not many people would know about and he has to explain how it works. He does think, though, that it will definitely "come into general use" and so predicts how popular it will be. So one text is about a new invention that is not yet very well known, and the other text is about a ten year old invention that everyone knows about and uses.

Paragraph C Source C tells you how popular the smartphone is with all kinds of people because children and teenagers use it all the time, grandparents use it to keep in touch with their grandchildren, parents use it to check what their children are doing and when they will be home, and lots of businesses use it for making deals and talking to each other. When the telephone was first invented though it was only popular with people who were doing demonstrations and with Queen Victoria so not many people used it. The biggest difference between the two inventions is how popular they are.

Suggested answer

I would include paragraph __B__ because it answers the question. It identifies a significant difference between the two inventions described in the two sources.

I would not include paragraphs __A__ or __C__ because paragraph A focuses on a similarity and is more about the writer's attitude to the invention than the invention itself. Paragraph C does not make a valid comparison because several references to both texts are inaccurate.

47

Answers

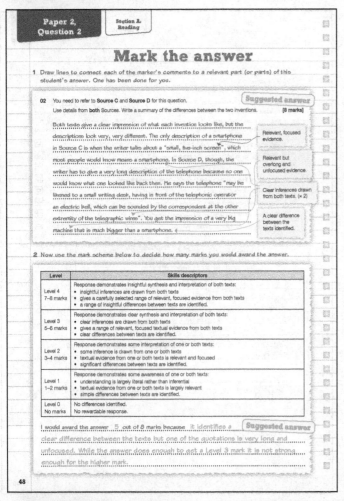

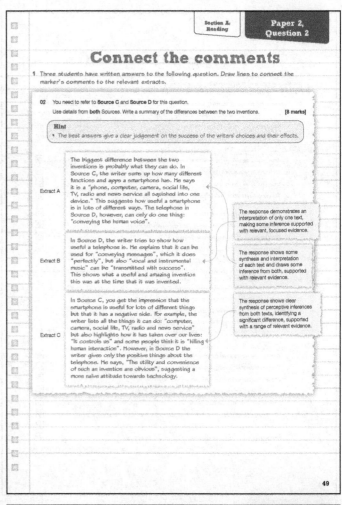

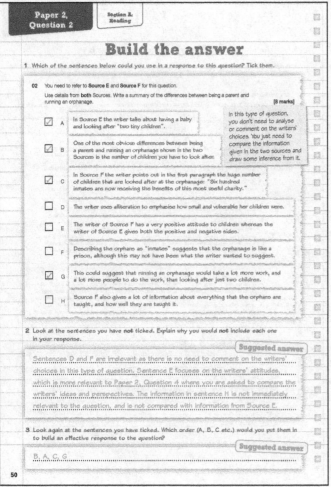

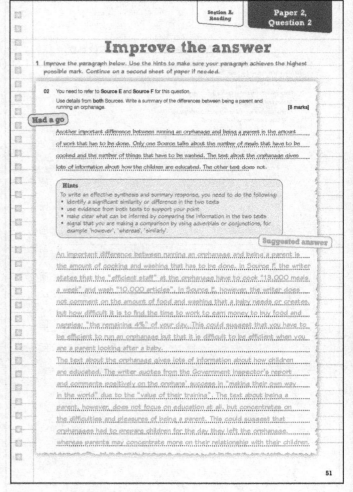

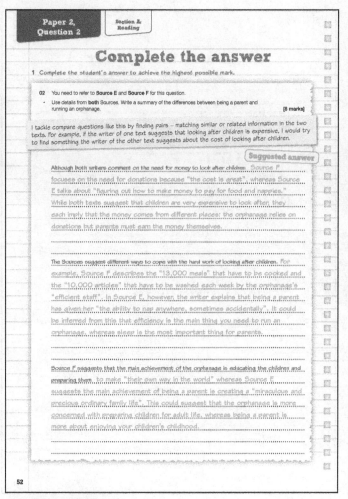

Complete the answer

1 Complete the student's answer to achieve the highest possible mark.

02 You need to refer to **Source E** and **Source F** for this question.
- Use details from **both** Sources. Write a summary of the differences between being a parent and running an orphanage. **[8 marks]**

I tackle compare questions like this by finding pairs – matching similar or related information in the two texts. For example, if the writer of one text suggests that looking after children is expensive, I would try to find something the writer of the other text suggests about the cost of looking after children.

Suggested answer

Although both writers comment on the need for money to look after children, Source F focuses on the need for donations because "the cost is great", whereas Source E talks about "figuring out how to make money to pay for food and nappies." While both texts suggest that children are very expensive to look after, they each imply that the money comes from different places: the orphanage relies on donations but parents must earn the money themselves.

The Sources suggest different ways to cope with the hard work of looking after children. For example, Source F describes the "13,000 meals" that have to be cooked and the "10,000 articles" that have to be washed each week by the orphanage's "efficient staff". In Source E, however, the writer explains that being a parent has given her "the ability to nap anywhere, sometimes accidentally". It could be inferred from this that efficiency is the main thing you need to run an orphanage, whereas sleep is the most important thing for parents.

Source F suggests that the main achievement of the orphanage is educating the children and preparing them to make "their own way in the world" whereas Source E suggests the main achievement of being a parent is creating a "miraculous and precious ordinary family life". This could suggest that the orphanage is more concerned with preparing children for adult life, whereas being a parent is more about enjoying your children's childhood.

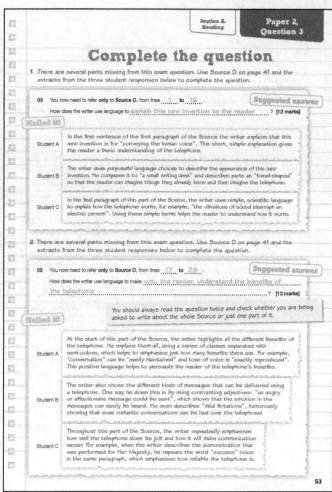

Complete the question

1 There are several parts missing from this exam question. Use Source D on page 41 and the extracts from the three student responses below to complete the question.

03 You now need to refer only to **Source D**, from lines __1__ to __16__. *Suggested answer*
How does the writer use language to _explain this new invention to the reader_? **[12 marks]**

Nailed it!

Student A In the first sentence of the first paragraph of the Source the writer explains that this new invention is for "conveying the human voice". This short, simple explanation gives the reader a basic understanding of the telephone.

Student B The writer uses purposeful language choices to describe the appearance of this new invention. He compares it to "a small writing desk" and describes parts as "funnel-shaped" so that the reader can imagine things they already know and then imagine the telephone.

Student C In the final paragraph of this part of the Source, the writer uses simple, scientific language to explain how the telephone works, for example, "the vibrations of sound interrupt an electric current". Using these simple terms helps the reader to understand how it works.

2 There are several parts missing from this exam question. Use Source D on page 41 and the extracts from the three student responses below to complete the question.

03 You now need to refer only to **Source D**, from lines __17__ to __28__. *Suggested answer*
How does the writer use language to make _you, the reader, understand the benefits of the telephone_? **[12 marks]**

Nailed it!

You should always read the question twice and check whether you are being asked to write about the whole Source or just one part of it.

Student A At the start of this part of the Source, the writer highlights all the different benefits of the telephone. He explains them all, using a series of clauses separated with semi-colons, which helps to emphasise just how many benefits there are. For example, "conversation" can be "easily maintained" and tone of voice is "exactly reproduced". This positive language helps to persuade the reader of the telephone's benefits.

Student B The writer also shows the different kinds of messages that can be delivered using a telephone. One way he does this is by using contrasting adjectives: "an angry or affectionate message could be sent", which shows that the emotion in the messages can easily be heard. He even describes "mild flirtations", humorously showing that even romantic conversations can be had over the telephone!

Student C Throughout this part of the Source, the writer repeatedly emphasises how well the telephone does its job and how it will make communication easier. For example, when the writer describes the demonstration that was performed for Her Majesty, he repeats the word "success" twice in the same paragraph, which emphasises how reliable the telephone is.

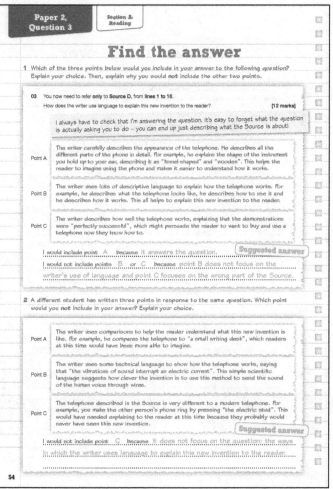

Find the answer

1 Which of the three points below would you include in your answer to the following question? Explain your choice. Then, explain why you would not include the other two points.

03 You now need to refer only to **Source D**, from lines 1 to 16.
How does the writer use language to explain this new invention to the reader? **[12 marks]**

I always have to check that I'm answering the question. It's easy to forget what the question is actually asking you to do – you can end up just describing what the Source is about!

Point A The writer carefully describes the appearance of the telephone. He describes all the different parts of the phone in detail. For example, he explains the shape of the instrument you hold up to your ear, describing it as "funnel-shaped" and "wooden". This helps the reader to imagine using the phone and makes it easier to understand how it works.

Point B The writer uses lots of descriptive language to explain how the telephone works. For example, he describes what the telephone looks like, he describes how to use it and he describes how it works. This all helps to explain this new invention to the reader.

Point C The writer describes how well the telephone works, explaining that the demonstrations were "perfectly successful", which might persuade the reader to want to buy and use a telephone now they know how to.

Suggested answer
I would include point A because it answers the question.
I would not include points B or C because point B does not focus on the writer's use of language and point C focuses on the wrong part of the Source.

2 A different student has written a point in response to the same question. Which point would you not include in your answer? Explain your choice.

Point A The writer uses comparisons to help the reader understand what this new invention is like. For example, he compares the telephone to "a small writing desk", which readers at this time would have been more able to imagine.

Point B The writer uses some technical language to show how the telephone works, saying that "the vibrations of sound interrupt an electric current". This simple scientific language suggests how clever the invention is to use this method to send the sound of the human voice through wires.

Point C The telephone described in the Source is very different to a modern telephone. For example, you make the other person's phone ring by pressing "the electric stud". This would have needed explaining to the reader at this time because they probably would never have seen this new invention.

Suggested answer
I would not include point C because it does not focus on the question: the ways in which the writer uses language to explain this new invention to the reader.

Mark the answer

1 Draw lines to connect each of the marker's comments to a relevant part of this student's answer. One has been done for you.

03 You now need to refer only to **Source D**, from lines 17 to 28. *Suggested answer*
How does the writer use language to make you, the reader, understand the benefits of the telephone? **[12 marks]**

The writer shows the benefits of the telephone by saying it is like a speaking tube "practically unlimited in length", which suggests that the power of the telephone is unlimited because it can deliver messages anywhere. The writer also describes the telephone as being "in its infancy", which suggests that the telephone is like a child that will grow and become much stronger. Beginning this sentence with the words "At present" suggests that this might happen soon.

Comments:
- Relevant evidence is used to support comments.
- A limited comment on language choice with little explanation or analysis.
- Comment on sentence form is limited but valid.
- A valid, developed comment on language choice, focused on its effect.
- An opportunity to use subject terminology is missed.

2 Now use the mark scheme below to decide how many marks you would award the answer.

Level	Skills descriptors
Level 4 10–12 marks	Response demonstrates a developed and insightful appreciation of the writer's use of language: • clear and detailed analysis of the effect of the writer's language choices • a carefully selected range of relevant, focused textual evidence • a range of subject terminology to achieve clarity and precision.
Level 3 7–9 marks	Response demonstrates clear appreciation of the writer's use of language: • clear comments on the effect of the writer's language choices • a range of relevant, focused textual evidence • a range of subject terminology to achieve clarity.
Level 2 4–6 marks	Response demonstrates some appreciation of the writer's use of language: • some comments on the effect of the writer's language choices • relevant and focused subject terminology • largely accurate subject terminology.
Level 1 1–3 marks	Response demonstrates some awareness of the writer's use of language: • straightforward comments on the effect of the writer's language choices • largely relevant textual evidence • some use of subject terminology, with inconsistent accuracy.
Level 0 No marks	No comments made on the writer's use of language. No rewardable response.

Suggested answer
I would award the answer 7 out of 12 marks because some of the comments on language are developed but others are limited, with little explanation or analysis.

Connect the comments

1 Three students have written answers to the following question. Draw lines to connect each of the marker's comments to the relevant extract.

> 03 You now need to refer **only** to **Source D**, from **lines 17 to 28**.
>
> How does the writer use language to make you, the reader, understand the benefits of the telephone? **[12 marks]**

> I always have to remind myself that long answers are not always better answers!

Extract A

Throughout the Source the writer uses positive adverbials to highlight the benefits of the telephone. The demonstration was "perfectly successful", conversations were "easily maintained" and the voices were "exactly reproduced", emphasising to the reader the fact that the telephone is simple to use and completely reliable.

The response shows some awareness of the writer's use of language and makes a straightforward comment on its effect, supported with relevant evidence. However, the response also summarises details from the Source without making any further comment on the writer's use of language.

Extract B

The writer compares the telephone with a telegraphic message to show how much better it is. The writer uses the phrases "time to write" and "a skilled operator" to show how complicated it is to send a telegraphic message. In contrast, the writer uses the verb "whisper" to show how easy it is to send a message using the telephone.

The response shows some appreciation of a range of the writer's language choices, selecting relevant focused evidence and accurately using subject terminology to comment on its effect. Comments could be developed to analyse the writer's use of language in more detail.

Extract C

The writer describes the way the telephone worked in the demonstration as "perfectly successful", which shows that the telephone works well and is a good invention. It also tells you how well it worked because it says the voices were clear and the two people on the phone could hear what the other person was saying and they could understand how the other person was feeling, which shows how clear their voices were and how well the telephone works.

This response shows a clear and developed appreciation of the writer's language choices, analysing their effect in detail, supported with a range of relevant focused evidence and accurate subject terminology.

Build the answer

1 Look at the question below and Source F on page 43. Which sentences would you use in your response? Tick them.

> 03 You now need to refer **only** to **Source F**, from **lines 1 to 18**.
>
> How does the writer use language to make you, the reader, feel you would like to help the orphans? **[12 marks]**

- [x] **A** In this part of the Source, the writer gives the reader the impression that the children in the orphanage are like angels but also very vulnerable.
- [ ] **B** The writer presents the orphans in a really positive way.
- [ ] **C** The writer uses lots of descriptive words to persuade the reader to give money to the orphanage.
- [x] **D** The writer uses alliteration to describe an orphan's "soft satin-skinned hand", which makes it sound very fragile, as though the child can easily be hurt and needs to be protected.
- [x] **E** The writer asks the reader to imagine meeting one of the babies and the "great thrill" that will run "through your heart" when you do. The noun "thrill" and the verb "runs" suggest how strongly you would feel sympathy and affection for the child.
- [x] **F** The writer highlights how small and vulnerable the orphans are, using the adjectives "tiny" and "little" to suggest that they need the reader's help.
- [x] **G** The overall impression the writer gives in this part of the Source is of a beautiful baby that needs your affection and your money.

2 Look at the sentences you have **not** ticked. Explain why you would **not** include each one in your response.

> **Suggested answer**
>
> Sentence B makes a valid point but is not as relevant to the rest of the paragraph as the point made in sentence A. Sentence C is vague and undeveloped, and does not provide specific examples; it is not relevant to the rest of the paragraph.

3 Look again at the sentences you have ticked. Which order (A, B, C etc.) would you put them in to build an effective response to the question?

> **Suggested answer**
>
> A, F, D, E, G

Re-order the answer

1 The paragraphs below are taken from a student's response to the following question. Rearrange the paragraphs into the most logical order by numbering them from 1 to 4.

> 03 You now need to refer **only** to **Source F**, from **lines 1 to 18**.
>
> How does the writer use language to make you, the reader, feel you would like to help the orphans? **[12 marks]**

> I always plan my answer by spending a minute noting down my ideas and putting them in the best order.

[4] Furthermore, the writer suggests how sorry you should feel for them. He says that the orphans would be interesting to "every sympathetic tender heart", using positive language choices to flatter the reader and make them want to feel sorry for the orphans and to help them. It makes you feel that if you are not interested and do not want to help them, you are different to everyone else and you are cruel.

[1] The writer begins the Source by writing about the kinds of children at the orphanage. He uses a long list to show all the different types of family the orphans come from, including "clergymen, officers in the army... doctors, lawyers". This suggests they come from rich parents whom they have now lost. This might make the reader feel sorry for them.

[3] The writer tries to appeal to the reader by describing the orphans in detail. He focuses on their "ringing voices", their "chubby arms" and their "soft satin-skinned hand". The word "ringing" suggests their voices make a musical noise, while their "soft satin" skin makes them sound precious but delicate. These adjectives are used to make the orphans sound as appealing as possible, and to make the reader feel sorry for them.

[2] At the end of this part of the Source, the writer again emphasises the number of different children the orphanage has helped using a statistic, explaining that "Two thousand three hundred and eighty-four little ones have entered that nursery" since it began. This emphasises how much good work the orphanage does and how much it needs your help.

2 Now, explain your choice.

> You can organise your answer by writing about each part, or each different idea in the Source in turn.

> **Suggested answer**
>
> The first two paragraphs comment on the type and number of children in the orphanage and so one logically follows the other. The third and fourth paragraphs both focus on the writer's presentation of the orphans and the response he hopes to create in the reader.

Complete the answer

1 Complete the student's answer to achieve the highest possible mark.

> 03 You now need to refer **only** to **Source F**, from **lines 19 to 28**.
>
> How does the writer use language to make you, the reader, feel you would like to make a donation to the orphanage? **[12 marks]**

> Highlight the language choices you want to comment on in the Source. Then you'll be able to see all the choices you want to comment on and find them much more quickly when you come to write your response.

> **Suggested answer**
>
> The writer quotes the Government Inspector focusing on very positive achievements highlighted with very positive adjectives, for example: "excellent... successful... valuable". This suggests to the reader that the money will be used well, so it is worthwhile making a donation.
>
> The writer describes the orphanage as "a grand baby-show" to suggest that it is a pleasure to visit the orphanage to see how well the children are looked after and to see how much they deserve your donation.
>
> The writer uses statistics to highlight how much work the orphanage does to help the children, for example: "13,000 meals a-week... washing the 10,000 articles that represent the laundry-work". The large scale of these numbers emphasises why the donation money is needed.
>
> The writer positions "for the cost is great" at the start of a sentence to emphasise this key point, highlighting how desperately the orphanage needs donations.

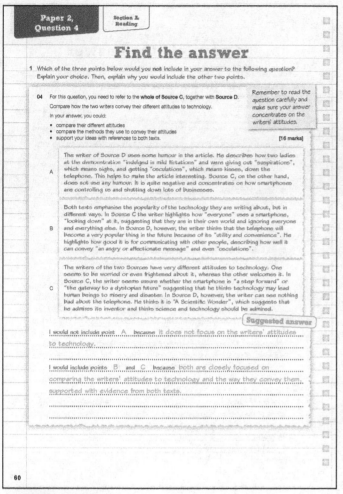

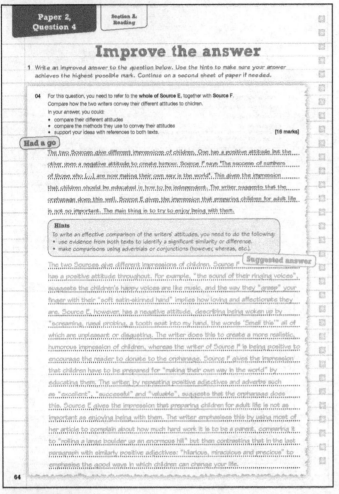

Paper 2, Question 4 — Section A: Reading

Improve the answer

1 Write an improved answer to the question below. Use the hints to make sure your answer achieves the highest possible mark. Continue on a second sheet of paper if needed.

04 For this question, you need to refer to the **whole of Source E**, together with **Source F**.
Compare how the two writers convey their different attitudes to children.
In your answer, you could:
• compare their different attitudes
• compare the methods they use to convey their attitudes
• support your ideas with references to both texts. [16 marks]

Had a go

The two Sources give different impressions of children. One has a positive attitude but the other uses a negative attitude to create humour. Source F says "The success of numbers of those who [...] are now making their own way in the world". This gives the impression that children should be educated in how to be independent. The writer suggests that the orphanage does this well. Source E gives the impression that preparing children for adult life is not so important. The main thing is to try to enjoy being with them.

Hints
To write an effective comparison of the writers' attitudes, you need to do the following:
• use evidence from both texts to identify a significant similarity or difference.
• make comparisons using adverbials or conjunctions (however, whereas, etc).

Suggested answer

The two Sources give different impressions of children. Source F has a positive attitude throughout. For example, "the sound of their ringing voices", suggests the children's happy voices are like music, and the way they "grasp" your finger with their "soft satin-skinned hand" implies how loving and affectionate they are. Source E, however, has a negative attitude, describing being woken up by "screaming, nasal probing, a tooth spat into my hand, the words 'Smell this'" all of which are unpleasant or disgusting. The writer does this to create a more realistic, humorous impression of children, whereas the writer of Source F is being positive to encourage the reader to donate to the orphanage. Source F gives the impression that children have to be prepared for "making their own way in the world" by educating them. The writer, by repeating positive adjectives and adverbs such as "excellent", "successful" and "valuable", suggests that the orphanage does this. Source E gives the impression that preparing children for adult life is not as important as enjoying being with them. The writer emphasises this by using most of her article to complain about how much hard work it is to be a parent, comparing it to "rolling a large boulder up an enormous hill" but then contrasting that in the last paragraph with similarly positive adjectives: "hilarious, miraculous and precious" to emphasise the good ways in which children can change your life.

64

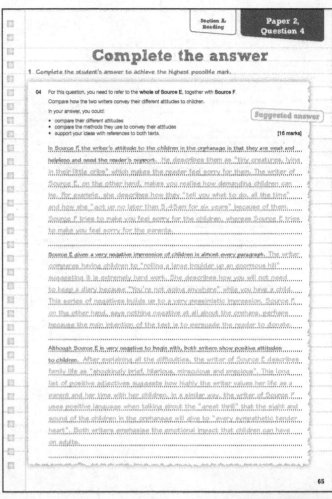

Section A: Reading — **Paper 2, Question 4**

Complete the answer

1 Complete the student's answer to achieve the highest possible mark.

04 For this question, you need to refer to the **whole of Source E**, together with **Source F**.
Compare how the two writers convey their different attitudes to children.
In your answer, you could:
• compare their different attitudes
• compare the methods they use to convey their attitudes
• support your ideas with references to both texts. [16 marks]

Suggested answer

In Source F, the writer's attitude to the children in the orphanage is that they are weak and helpless and need the reader's support. He describes them as, "tiny creatures, lying in their little cribs" which makes the reader feel sorry for them. The writer of Source E, on the other hand, makes you realise how demanding children can be. For example, she describes how they "tell you what to do, all the time" and how she "got up no later than 5.45am for six years" because of them. Source F tries to make you feel sorry for the children, whereas Source E tries to make you feel sorry for the parents.

Source E gives a very negative impression of children in almost every paragraph. The writer compares having children to "rolling a large boulder up an enormous hill", suggesting it is extremely hard work. She describes how you will not need to keep a diary because "You're not going anywhere", while you have a child. This series of negatives builds up to a very pessimistic impression. Source F, on the other hand, says nothing negative at all about the orphans, perhaps because the main intention of the text is to persuade the reader to donate.

Although Source E is very negative to begin with, both writers show positive attitudes to children. After explaining all the difficulties, the writer of Source E describes family life as "shockingly brief, hilarious, miraculous and precious". This long list of positive adjectives suggests how highly the writer values her life as a parent and her time with her children. In a similar way, the writer of Source F uses positive language when talking about the "great thrill" that the sight and sound of the children in the orphanage will give to "every sympathetic tender heart". Both writers emphasise the emotional impact that children can have on adults.

65

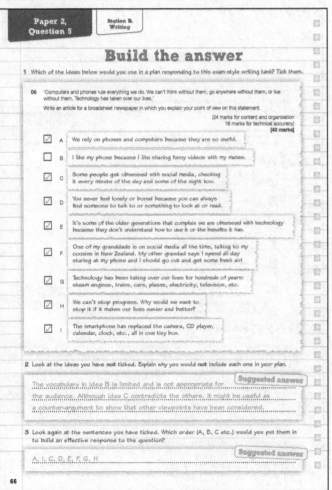

Paper 2, Question 5 — Section B: Writing

Build the answer

1 Which of the ideas below would you use in a plan responding to this exam-style writing task? Tick them.

05 'Computers and phones rule everything we do. We can't think without them, go anywhere without them, or live without them. Technology has taken over our lives.'
Write an article for a broadsheet newspaper in which you explain your point of view on this statement.
(24 marks for content and organisation
16 marks for technical accuracy)
[40 marks]

☑ A We rely on phones and computers because they are so useful.

☐ B I like my phone because I like sharing funny videos with my mates.

☑ C Some people get obsessed with social media, checking it every minute of the day and some of the night too.

☑ D You never feel lonely or bored because you can always find someone to talk to or something to look at or read.

☑ E It's some of the older generations that complain we are obsessed with technology because they don't understand how to use it or the benefits it has.

☑ F One of my granddads is on social media all the time, talking to my cousins in New Zealand. My other grandad says I spend all day staring at my phone and I should go out and get some fresh air!

☑ G Technology has been taking over our lives for hundreds of years: steam engines, trains, cars, planes, electricity, television, etc.

☑ H We can't stop progress. Why would we want to stop it if it makes our lives easier and better?

☑ I The smartphone has replaced the camera, CD player, calendar, clock, etc., all in one tiny box.

2 Look at the ideas you have **not** ticked. Explain why you would **not** include each one in your plan.

Suggested answer

The vocabulary in idea B is limited and is not appropriate for the audience. Although idea C contradicts the others, it might be useful as a counter-argument to show that other viewpoints have been considered.

3 Look again at the sentences you have ticked. Which order (A, B, C etc.) would you put them in to build an effective response to the question?

Suggested answer

A, I, G, D, E, F, C, H

66

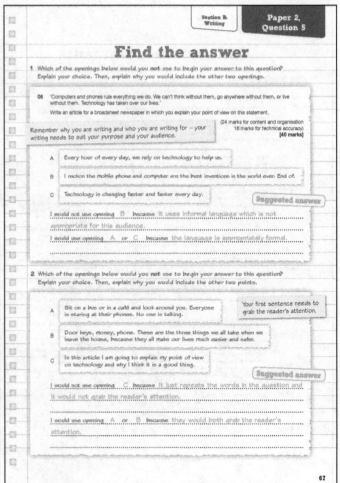

Section B: Writing — **Paper 2, Question 5**

Find the answer

1 Which of the openings below would you **not** use to begin your answer to this question? Explain your choice. Then, explain why you would include the other two openings.

05 'Computers and phones rule everything we do. We can't think without them, go anywhere without them, or live without them. Technology has taken over our lives.'
Write an article for a broadsheet newspaper in which you explain your point of view on this statement.
(24 marks for content and organisation
16 marks for technical accuracy)
[40 marks]

Remember why you are writing and who you are writing for – your writing needs to suit your purpose and your audience.

A Every hour of every day, we rely on technology to help us.

B I reckon the mobile phone and computer are the best inventions in the world ever! End of.

C Technology is changing faster and faster every day.

Suggested answer

I would not use opening B because it uses informal language which is not appropriate for this audience.

I would use opening A or C because the language is appropriately formal.

2 Which of the openings below would you **not** use to begin your answer to this question? Explain your choice. Then, explain why you would include the other two points.

A Sit on a bus or in a café and look around you. Everyone is staring at their phones. No one is talking.

Your first sentence needs to grab the reader's attention.

B Door keys, money, phone. These are the three things we all take when we leave the house, because they all make our lives much easier and safer.

C In this article I am going to explain my point of view on technology and why I think it is a good thing.

Suggested answer

I would not use opening C because it just repeats the words in the question and it would not grab the reader's attention.

I would use opening A or B because they would both grab the reader's attention.

67

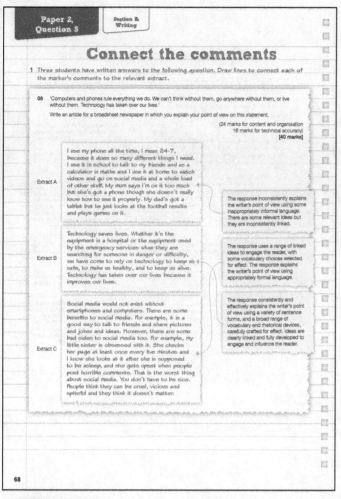

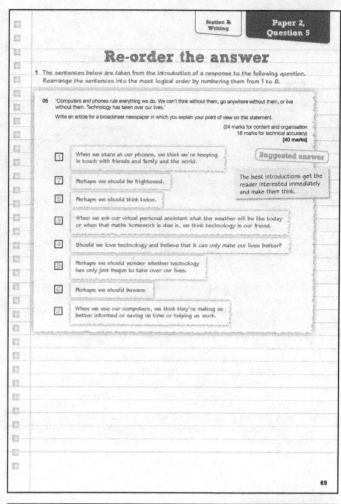

Mark the answer

1 Draw lines to connect each of the marker's comments to a relevant part of this student's answer. One has been done for you.

05 'Computers and phones rule everything we do. We can't think without them, go anywhere without them, or live without them. Technology has taken over our lives.'

Write an article for a broadsheet newspaper in which you explain your point of view on this statement.

(24 marks for content and organisation
16 marks for technical accuracy)
[40 marks]

Suggested answer

I lost my phone for a day once and I spent hours and hours looking for it and I couldn't find it anywhere and I realised how much I use it and need it and I felt kind of lost without it. It shows how much we need phones and technology and how we've got used to having them and we can't live without them.

- A relevant key point is made based on personal experience but it is not developed.
- Informal language choice is inappropriate for the task.
- Repetitive sentence structure weakens the impact of the writer's ideas.
- Vocabulary is limited, expressing ideas clearly but with little impact.

2 Draw lines to connect each of the marker's comments to a relevant part of this student's answer.

Suggested answer

We often think of technology as being something that is used only by young people, organising their social lives, talking to their vast group of friends, sharing photos and videos. However, technology can help the lonely, the isolated and the elderly by giving them a direct line to the rest of the world. A grandmother living on her own can chat to her grandchildren on the other side of the world. An elderly man can text his shopping list to a friendly, helpful neighbour who can order it online and get it delivered, then chat to his friend from the old days who lives hundreds of miles away, or in a different country. Technology can help us all, young and old.

- A developed key point clearly explains the writer's point of view.
- A range of examples support the writer's point of view.
- The writer's point of view is expressed clearly and precisely through careful vocabulary choices.
- Short sentence form gives emphasis to the writer's point of view.

Build the answer

1 Look at this question and the student's sentences below. Which sentences would you use in the main section of a response to this question? Tick them.

05 'Computers and phones rule everything we do. We can't think without them, go anywhere without them, or live without them. Technology has taken over our lives.'

Write an article for a broadsheet newspaper in which you explain your point of view on this statement.

(24 marks for content and organisation
16 marks for technical accuracy)
[40 marks]

- [✓] A I think technology is killing our ability to communicate with each other.
- [✓] B People often say that technology helps us communicate more effectively with each other.
- [✓] C Sometimes my friends message me on my phone when we are in the same room.
- [✓] D My sister messages my mum from her room, asking her to bring her some food or a drink.
- [ ] E Amazingly, my mum actually takes her the food or the drink!
- [✓] F Simple conversations, manners and politeness, kindness and thoughtfulness have all been replaced with a short, cold message on a screen.
- [✓] G Nobody sends birthday cards anymore, except my grandma and even she is starting to use social media.
- [✓] H Instead of talking and laughing together, we just press buttons.
- [✓] I Which would you rather do: type LOL on a screen or actually laugh out loud with your friends or family, together, in the same room?

2 Look at the sentences you have not ticked. Explain why you would not include each one in your answer.

Suggested answer
Sentence E is a distraction from the topic and does not support the writer's viewpoint.

3 Look again at the sentences you have ticked. Which order (A, B, C etc.) would you put them in to build an effective response to the question?

Suggested answer
B, A, C, D, G, F, H, I

Answers

Improve the answer

1. Write an improved answer to the question below. Use the hints to make sure your answer achieves the highest possible mark. Continue on a second sheet of paper if needed.

05 'Computers and phones rule everything we do. We can't think without them, go anywhere without them, or live without them. Technology has taken over our lives.'

Write an article for a broadsheet newspaper in which you explain your point of view on this statement.

(24 marks for content and organisation
16 marks for technical accuracy)
[40 marks]

Had a go

Everyone has got a phone and a computer. Everyone uses them all the time. If they weren't useful, nobody would buy them or use them. Some people say we should turn our phones off every now and then, but I disagree.

Hints

To present your point of view, each paragraph in the main body of your writing needs to do the following:
- make a developed key point that will help to explain your point of view
- use evidence to support the key point – this could be a fact, or an example from your own experience
- clearly explain how this point and evidence support your point of view, helping the reader to understand and agree with your point of view.
There are three opportunities for improvement in the first paragraph: the key point, the evidence and the explanation could all be more fully developed.

Suggested answer

Everyone has a phone and a computer because they are an essential part of modern life. Everyone uses them all the time as they make almost every task easier and quicker. For example, if you wanted to write to a friend or relation before the internet was invented, you would have to write a letter, take it to the letter box and post it, and it would take at least a day to arrive. Now you can send a message from the sofa in less than ten seconds. If technology was not useful, nobody would buy it or use it. Technology has not taken over our lives. It's made our lives better.

Some people say we should turn our phones off every now and then. They argue that checking your phone for texts, social media posts and everything else that pops up on a smartphone can make you addicted, causing you to stop interacting with your friends in real life or to stay awake half the night. However, I disagree. The whole point of a smartphone is that it keeps you connected with the world. You do not have to turn it off – you can just ignore it or put it on silent if you have something more interesting or important to do.

72

Connect the comments

1. Three students have written answers to the following question. Draw lines to connect each of the marker's comments to the relevant conclusion.

05 'Computers and phones rule everything we do. We can't think without them, go anywhere without them, or live without them. Technology has taken over our lives.'

Write an article for a broadsheet newspaper in which you explain your point of view on this statement.

(24 marks for content and organisation
16 marks for technical accuracy)
[40 marks]

Don't just repeat your main ideas in your conclusion. You need to summarise your point of view and explain the benefits of agreeing with it. You could also explain the problems people will face if they ignore your point of view!

Conclusion A

Technology helps us to communicate, it helps us to look after ourselves and it helps us to look after each other. We can use it to find out about the world and to change the world. It informs us, it entertains us, and it brings us closer together. If technology has all these benefits, why should we worry that it is playing such a big part in our lives? Technology is our slave, not our master.

There is a limited sense of reaching a conclusion in this final paragraph. Although it makes the writer's point of view clear, it simply repeats key points already made in the main body of the article and does not develop them. A limited range of vocabulary and sentence forms reduces its impact.

Conclusion B

As I have already said, technology can be a good thing but it can also be a bad thing. It can help us in our lives but if we use it too much we will have to rely on it for everything we do and, as I said earlier, what happens if it goes wrong? Overall, I think technology is a good thing but we should not rely on it too much.

The writer introduces a new idea in this conclusion, summarising earlier ideas about technology to consider its role in the future. A limited range of vocabulary reduces the impact of the writer's point of view, although there is some use of sentence forms for effect.

Conclusion C

Technology may have many advantages and there are lots of things it can do. However, we should always think about the negative effects it can have on our lives. As technology develops in the future, there may be many more negative effects and problems we cannot imagine, for example computers developing minds of their own and taking over. I think we should be careful.

This conclusion effectively summarises the writer's key ideas, making effective use of a variety of vocabulary and sentence forms for effect. The final sentences engage the reader, encouraging a response in agreement with the writer's view.

73

Improve the answer

1. Improve the paragraph below. Use the hints to make sure your paragraph achieves the highest possible mark. Continue on a second sheet of paper if needed.

05 'Computers and phones rule everything we do. We can't think without them, go anywhere without them, or live without them. Technology has taken over our lives.'

Write an article for a broadsheet newspaper in which you explain your point of view on this statement.

(24 marks for content and organisation
16 marks for technical accuracy)
[40 marks]

Nearly there

Everything would be different without technology. Imagine it. First, you wake up late because you haven't got an alarm. You don't even have a phone to tell your boss or friend you're going to be late for work or school. How are you supposed to get there quickly when there are no cars? You need to find another way to get to work but you can't look it up because there is no internet. So you walk to school, sit in lessons while the teacher talks at you because there are no computers or videos. Then you walk home and look at the walls because there is nothing else to do. Everything is better with technology.

Hints

To present your point of view effectively and engage your reader, think about the vocabulary you choose and how you can use language devices to give additional impact to your ideas. For example, you could use the following features:
- emotive language
- alliteration
- rhetorical questions
- lists or triple structures.

Suggested answer

Can you imagine how dramatically different life would be without technology? Think about it. You wake up late in the morning panicking because you haven't got an alarm. You urgently need to tell your friend you're going to be late for work or school but you can't because you haven't got a phone. You desperately need to get to school or work quickly but you can't because there are no cars. You need to find a way to get to work but you can't look it up because there is no internet. So you plod the miles and miles to school, sit fidgeting in lessons while the teacher drones on and on at you because there are no computers to help you learn or videos to help you understand. Then you plod all the way home again and stare at the walls, dying of boredom because there is nothing else to do. Everything is faster, simpler, better with technology.

74

Mark the answer

1. Draw lines to connect each of the marker's comments to a relevant part (or parts) of this student's answer. One has been done for you.

05 'Computers and phones rule everything we do. We can't think without them, go anywhere without them, or live without them. Technology has taken over our lives.'

Write an article for a broadsheet newspaper in which you explain your point of view on this statement.

(24 marks for content and organisation
16 marks for technical accuracy)
[40 marks]

Suggested answer

A recent survey showed that teenagers would rather give up choclate than give up their phones for a week, and it also showed that the average teenager spends up to six hours a day on their phones, this shows how much their lives are ruled by technology. If there was more for teenagers to do then they probably would not spend so much time staring at their phones. They might go out and enjoy themselves and get some fresh air.

A limited range of sentence forms are used.

Full stops and other sentence demarcation are not consistently accurate. (You only need to provide one example of this.)

Vocabulary choices are somewhat varied. (x 2)

Spelling of some common words is inaccurate. (x 3)

2. Draw lines to connect each of the marker's comments to a relevant part (or parts) of this student's answer. One has been done for you.

Suggested answer

Technology is designed to take over our lives. If you have ever played a console or computer game, you will know how hours can last seconds and whole days can disappear as you battle against aliens or enemy soldiers or cartoon characters in cars. Games are made for addiction. However, how many hours did we spend playing games before technology took over? A simple game of Monopoly can last an entire afternoon. My dad can spend half an hour staring at a chess board, trying to decide which little wooden figure to move a whole square forward – and that's just one move in a game that can last a whole day. Technology hasn't taken over our lives. It's just changed the things we do and the way we do them.

A range of sentence forms are crafted for effect.

Full stops and other sentence demarcation are accurate. (You only need to provide one example of this.)

A broad range of vocabulary choices. (x 2)

Spelling of some words is inaccurate.

75

92

Notes

Published by Pearson Education Limited, 80 Strand, London, WC2R 0RL.

www.pearsonschools.co.uk

Text © Pearson Education Limited 2018
Edited, typeset and produced by Elektra Media Ltd
Original illustrations © Pearson Education Limited 2018
Illustrated by Elektra Media Ltd
Cover illustration by Miriam Sturdee

The right of David Grant to be identified as author of this work has been asserted by him in accordance with the Copyright, Designs and Patents Act 1988.

First published 2018

21 20 19 18
10 9 8 7 6 5 4 3 2 1

British Library Cataloguing in Publication Data
A catalogue record for this book is available from the British Library.

ISBN 978 1 292 23022 1

Acknowledgements
The author and publisher would like to thank the following individuals and organisations for their kind permission to reproduce copyright material:

Extract on page 4, 6, 7, 9, 10, 11, 15, 16, 17, 21, 22, 23, 24, 76: *The Illustrated Man* by Ray Bradbury © 2012, reproduced with the permission of Abner Stein; Extract on page 5, 8, 12, 18, 25, 77, 78, 79: *Quite Early One Morning* by Dylan Thomas © 1954, reproduced with the permission of New Directions Publishing Corp, and *The Collected Poems of Dylan Thomas: The Centenary Edition* by Dylan Thomas, reproduced with the permission of Weidenfeld & Nicolson; Extract on page 40, 47, 48, 49, 60, 61, 62, 85, 86: The Independent 2018; Extract on page 41, 47, 48, 49, 53, 54, 55, 56, 60, 61, 62: reproduced by kind permission of the The Field; Extract on page 42, 43, 50, 63, 87, 90: Copyright Guardian News & Media Ltd 2017.

Photographs
(Key: b-bottom; c-centre; l-left; r-right; t-top)

123RF: Andreiuc 88 28, 29, 30, 31, 32, 33, 82tl, 82tr, 82bl, 82br, 83l, 83r. **Shutterstock:** Vlad Teodor 40, Sergey Mironov 42.

All other images © Pearson Education

We would like to thank Joni Sommerville, Theo Mellors, Emily Plenty, John-Paul Duddy, Emily Atkinson, Jess Salmon, Holly Coop, Matthew Foot and David Birch for their invaluable help in providing student tips for the series.

Note from publisher
Pearson has robust editorial processes, including answer and fact checks, to ensure the accuracy of the content in this publication, and every effort is made to ensure this publication is free of errors. We are, however, only human, and occasionally errors do occur. Pearson is not liable for any misunderstandings that arise as a result of errors in this publication, but it is our priority to ensure that the content is accurate. If you spot an error, please do contact us at resourcescorrections@pearson.com so we can make sure it is corrected.